# THE KOREAN HOME KITCHEN

Traditional Home-Style Recipes That Capture the Flavors and Memories of

Korea | Full-color Picture Premium Edition

**BAEK MEE-YON**

**Copyright© 2022 By Baek Mee-Yon Rights Reserved**

This book is copyright protected. It is only for personal use. You cannot amend, distribute, sell, use, quote or paraphrase any part of the content within this book, without the consent of the author or publisher.

Under no circumstances will any blame or legal responsibility be held against the publisher, or author, for any damages, reparation, or monetary loss due to the information contained within this book, either directly or indirectly.

**Disclaimer Notice:**

Please note the information contained within this document is for educational and entertainment purposes only. All effort has been executed to present accurate, up to date, reliable, complete information. No warranties of any kind are declared or implied. Readers acknowledge that the author is not engaged in the rendering of legal, financial, medical or professional advice. The content within this book has been derived from various sources. Please consult a licensed professional before attempting any techniques outlined in this book.

By reading this document, the reader agrees that under no circumstances is the author responsible for any losses, direct or indirect, that are incurred as a result of the use of the information contained within this document, including, but not limited to, errors, omissions, or inaccuracies.

# Table of Contents

**Introduction** ... 1

**Chapter 1**
**Basics of Korean Food** ... 2
History of Korean Food ... 3
Ancient Food Fermentation ... 3
Temple Food From Korea ... 4

**Chapter 2**
**Start your Journey to Korean Food** ... 6
Korean Table Settings ... 7
Korean Foods and Dishes ... 7

**Chapter 3**
**Basic Stocks, Sauces, and Marinades** ... 9
Beef Stock ... 10
Sensational Soy Dipping Sauce ... 10
Chojang (Vinegar Gochujang Sauce) ... 10
Sweet and Spicy Dipping Sauce ... 10
Seasoned Soy Sauce ... 10
Vegetable Dipping Sauce ... 10
Korean Chili Sauce ... 11
Green Onion and Vinegar Sauce ... 11

**Chapter 4**
**Kimchi** ... 12
Napa Cabbage Kimchi ... 13
Cubed Radish Kimchi ... 13
Stuffed Cucumber Kimchi ... 14
Tomato Kimchi ... 14
Scallion Kimchi ... 14
Sliced Radish and Cabbage Water Kimchi ... 15
Garlic Chive Kimch ... 15
Whole Radish Water Kimchi ... 15
Perilla Kimchi ... 16
Salted Preserved Squid In Spicy Sauce ... 16

**Chapter 5**
**Banchan and Sides** ... 17
Steamed Eggs ... 18
Seasoned Rice Balls ... 18
Braised Lotus Root ... 18
Braised Potatoes ... 19
Steamed Eggplant ... 19
Stir-Fried Fish Cake ... 20
Seasoned Spinach ... 20
Spicy Cucumber Salad ... 21
Korean Lettuce Salad ... 22
Spicy Braised Tofu ... 23

**Chapter 6**
**The Main Event** ... 24
Classic Korean Beef ... 25
Southern-Style Beef Rib Patties ... 26
Pork Ribs With Garlic, Pear & Jujube ... 27

Spicy Pork Stir-Fry ... 28
Korean Sweet & Sour Pork ... 29
Chuncheon-Style Spicy Chicken Stir-Fry ... 30
Andong-Style Braised Chicken with Noodles ... 31
Korean Chicken Salad ... 32
Spicy Seafood & Bean Sprouts ... 33

**Chapter 7**
**Fish and Seafood** ... 34
Spicy Marinated Crabs ... 35
Pan-Fried Fish Fillets ... 36
Spicy Marinated Squid ... 37
Rice & Fish Lettuce Wraps ... 38
Marinated Shrimp ... 39
Crab Cakes in Korea ... 40
Spicy Shrimp Skewers ... 41

**Chapter 8**
**Soups, Stews & Braises** ... 42
Ground Soybean Stew ... 43
Braised Kimchi and Pork Belly ... 44
Rice Cake Soup ... 45
Oxtail Soup ... 46
Kimchi Stew ... 47
Seaweed Soup ... 48

**Chapter 9**
**Barbecue: Grilled, Smoked & Fired** ... 49
Octopus ... 50
Shrimp and Squid ... 51
BBQ Pork Belly ... 52
Braised Pork Belly ... 53
Beef and Tofu Meatballs ... 54
Marinated Skirt Steak ... 55
BBQ Beef Short Ribs ... 56
Roasted Cauliflower ... 57
BBQ King Oyster Mushrooms ... 58

**Chapter 10**
**Sweets, Desserts and Drinks** ... 59
Sweet Pancakes With Cinnamon Brown Sugar Filling ... 60
Watermelon Punch ... 60
Korean Cinnamon Punch ... 60
Cinnamon-Sugar Rice Cakes ... 61
No-Churn Korean Instant Coffee Ice Cream ... 61

**Appendix 1 Measurement Conversion Chart** ... 62
**Appendix 2 The Dirty Dozen and Clean Fifteen** ... 63
**Appendix 3 Index** ... 64

# Introduction

A Comprehensive Cookbook for Traditional Korean Cooking will show you how to incorporate the beauty of Korean cuisine inside your kitchen right away! Do you want to discover how to make Korean food yet are concerned that it could be too challenging? Do you want to know how to cook tasty, Asian-inspired food for you and your family while adding diversity to your meal options? Do you need a complete cookbook with traditional Korean dishes?

This cookbook is for you if your response to one of the above is yes.

With the help of the precise directions in this unique cookbook, you can discover how to prepare a variety of dishes, including Korean favorites like spicy noodle dishes, Tteok-Bok, ki Gukbap, and much more. You'll also be able to wow your family and friends with your culinary expertise. This cookbook will demonstrate how to savor the flavors of Korea in several interesting methods. Even if you have no expertise in Korean cuisine, this book will allow you to create a fast dinner on your own or organize a Korean-themed banquet for your friends and family.

# Chapter 1
# Basics of Korean Food

Korean food combines agricultural and nomadic traditions in Korea and Southern Manchuria. It is mainly based on seafood, meats, vegetables, and rice. The ingredients commonly used in cooking are paste made of fermented beans, red chili, salt, garlic, ginger, soy sauce, tomato sauce, black pepper, chili flakes, and napa cabbage.

## History of Korean Food

Korean food has its origin in China. For example, rice first originated in China, as did cabbages. Historically, Koreans enjoyed harvesting, sowing, farming, preparing food, and eating. These activities were known to the central part of their social events. These people used to live in villages outside their cities. Eating used to be the central part of their day. Koreans always used to sit together in clusters and have their meals.

Korean cuisine was divided into two parts- Royal cuisine and farmer's cuisine. Royal cuisine took a few hours to several days to prepare, and the poorer farmers used to cook within minutes. This constituted a significant difference between the two.

## Ancient Food Fermentation

Fermentation is a biological mechanism that preserves food and is used in much of ancient Korean cuisine. Jeotgal gochujang, ganjang, and Doenjang are some of the Korean dishes that best exemplify fermentation that formed part of the culture through which Korea has evolved. A few months to many decades might pass while the fermentation occurs.

## Temple Food From Korea

To offer the nutrients that the nuns and monks needed to be strong while abstaining from fleshly meat, Korean Buddhist monasteries developed meals that used a variety of vegetables. Vegans and those who adhere to specific diets can now too enjoy temple cooking.

Buddhist philosophy, which strongly focuses on wellness, simplicity, and concern for the environment, impacts the fundamentals of Korean temple food. Zero waste and Veganism practices have been followed by Korean monks and have run for more than 1600 years. Since then, Buddhist culinary customs have influenced much of contemporary Korean food. Korean temple cuisine emphasizes the use of sustainably obtained regional products. It focuses on vegan meals that require few ingredients and are environmentally beneficial.

Korean temple cuisine does not include fried chicken or barbecue. Instead, it offers nutritious, flavorful dishes like kimchi, tofu stews, steamed rice wrapped in lotus leaves, and rice soups.

The temple food diet requires a disciplined mentality since the food is so restricted. Buddhism forbids meat consumption; hence milk products are the only animal items used in Korean temple cuisine. As a result of the Buddhist belief that certain veggies obstruct religious experience, the nuns and monks are also forbidden from using the following five aromatic veggies: green onions, leeks, chives, garlic, and onion. Fermented, preserved, and natural food are the three kinds of foods consumed at Korean temples. For further detail on these three foods, see the following:

**ORGANIC FOOD**

The five acrid veggies are forbidden to safeguard Buddhist followers from potential interruptions while meditating. This ban also stops practitioners from falling in love with the flavor of solid spices, which might later disrupt their practice. A vegan culture has emerged in Korean temple cuisine due to the usage of various mountain flora and natural greens in place of synthetic tastes. Most Korean temples are situated in mountainous regions, where it is easy to get fresh, raw fruits, flowers, stems, leaves, and roots. Korean temple cuisine employs organic spices and taste enhancers instead of the usual spices we use, including raw kelp powder, mushroom powder, perilla seed powder, Jae-pi powder, and bean powder.

**PRESERVED FOOD**

Many types of veggies and crops are accessible in the winter in Korea, one of their four distinct seasons. The healthy flora and veggies have been preserved using various methods by nuns and monks for such winters. These items may be utilized for an extended period during the off-season while keeping their nutritional value, which is an advantage of preservation.

**FERMENTED FOODS**

The cuisine served at Korean temples differs from that served in the West. For instance, yogurt, wine, and cheese have become the usual fermented foods in the western region; however, Korea's fermented foods are red chili pepper paste, pine needle tea, rice punch, vinegar, and soy sauce.

Food is fermented, which gives it a delicious flavor, reduces cholesterol, contains cancer-preventive elements, and offers protection from age-related illnesses.

**ONDOL KITCHEN**

Korean home cooking has also been affected by advancements in construction and the diffusion of heating technologies from aristocratic residences to typical households. The shift from communal to private house kitchens was brought about by the rising popularity of ondol heating, a technique for warming a home's flooring. The development of cooking utensils might be placed well over exhaust apertures for wood (and subsequently charcoal) central heating.

Many additional culinary innovations were made feasible by modern developments like refrigeration, the invention of gas cooking and heating, and worldwide trade, leading to the current vibrant and intricate Korean cuisine.

# Chapter 2
# Start your Journey to Korean Food

## Korean Table Settings

Traditional Koreans used to sit in a squat position for their meals. The food used to be placed on a low table, whereas Urban Koreans followed western style seating arrangements. Jeotgarak, commonly known as silver or stainless steel chopsticks, and Sutgarak (a shallow spoon with a long handle) form the central part of meals. Koreans use chopsticks for eating banchan. Hot soup and steamed rice form the central part of a Korean meal.

As for drinks, Koreans usually drink chilled water with meals. Sometimes alcohol also accompanies their meals. After their cuisine, patrons drink sikhye or soo jung gwa. Regarding tea, Koreans drink grain tea, like barley tea.

## Korean Foods and Dishes

Korean cuisine is known for its spicy taste and sharp odor. Korean cuisine mainly depends on fermented food for its tangy and salty flavor.

**MAIN MEAT DISHES**

Include bulgogi , galbi, jokbal, samgyeopsal, hoe, sannakji, makchang, gobchang.

1. Bulgogi literally translates to "fire meat" and includes variations like pork, chicken, and squid.
2. Galbi is known for its spicy taste, and visitors call it Korean BBQ.
3. Jokbal includes the feet of a pig cooked with a shrimp sauce.
4. Samgyeopsal is served wrapped in lettuce leaves and grilled with garlic and onions.
5. Hoe is a seafood dish served raw, dipped in soy sauce with hot radish paste and sesame leaves.
6. Sannakji is a live octopus moving on the plate.
7. Makchang is a slice of pork grilled for its delicious taste and served with doenjang sauce.
8. Gobchang is similar to Makchang.

**ROYAL DISHES**

1. Gujeolpan is a plate with nine sections consisting of a variety of veggies, meats, and pancakes and is mainly served on special occasions like royal weddings and parties.
2. Sinseollo is a dish that includes meat and veggies cooked in rich soup. It is served in a silver bowl with a hole in the center and placed on a lump of burning coal or wood so that it can remain hot throughout the meal.

**SOUPS AND STEWS**

1. Doenjang jjigae is a soup made from soybean paste. It contains a variety of veggies, tofu, and shellfish.
2. Cheonggukjang jjigae is made of solid odor soybean paste.

3. Gamjatang is very spicy and made from the spice of pork and veggies.
4. Haejangguk is made in beef soup consisting of cabbage, pork spine, ox blood, and veggies.
5. Janchi guksu is based on soupy noodles.
6. Jeongol is a very delicious and spicy stew, served hot and consisting of seafood and veggies.
7. Kimchi jjigae is made from pork, tofu, and kimchi.
8. Maeuntang is a spicy fish soup.

**MIXED RICE**

1. Bibimbap is rice mixed with cooked veggies, beef, and egg and is served with chili paste.
2. Hoedeopbap is rice mixed with fish and veggies.

**BANCHAN**

This means side dishes. It includes

1. Kimchi is a fermented dish made from veggies like cabbage, radish, or cucumber soaked in salt water, accompanied by ginger, garlic, green onion, and chilies.
2. Kongnamul are sprouts of soybean which are healthy and rich in taste.

**NOODLES**

1. Naengmyeon is a cold noodle served in chilled soup with raw veggies and fruits. Sometimes it is also mixed with cold beef and boiled egg.
2. Japchae is made from potato noodles, veggies, sliced onions, and carrots (roasted) with soy sauce, half-refined sugar, and sesame oil.
3. Jajangmyeon is made from noodles and is served like pizza.
4. Kalguksu is boiled flat noodles served with anchovies and zucchini.

**DESSERTS**

1. Tteok is a cake-like chewing gum made from rice and is filled with sweet mung bean paste, raisins, sesame seeds, sweet pumpkin, dates, peanuts, and honey.
2. Songpyeon is a rice cake served at the Mid-Autumn festival, also known as Korean Thanksgiving. The dessert is often decorated with a pine stick.
3. Yakshik is made with sweet rice, jujube, chestnut, pinenut, and raw sugar.
4. Chapssaltteok is a rice cake filled with sweet bean paste.

Korean Beverages include insam cha, saenggang cha, sikhye, yujacha, bori cha, hyeonmi, and sungnyung.

Alcoholic Beverages include soju (the best-known liquor in Korea), cass, white, cafe, OB lager beer, and microbrewery.

As far as eating habits are concerned, Koreans eat very fast because they follow their pali culture. Pali means hurry and is linked with the country's fast economic development.
Before meals, Koreans usually say "Jal meokkesseumnida"; after meals, they say "Jal meokkesseumnida."

Koreans usually use metal utensils because they are more hygienic than others, and they are easy to clean at high temperatures.

As per the timing of meals, Koreans eat lunch between 12 pm and 1 pm, and dinner is between 18:30 pm to 22:00 pm.

Korean foods are generally considered healthy owing to their ingredients, like lots of veggies and limited oil.

Korean cookbooks include a vast collection of recipes, preparation methods, and serving suggestions to make your dishes look even more delicious. Korean cookbooks help beginners and lovers of Korean dishes make these delightful and mouth-watering cuisines in minutes. These books represent all kinds of Korean dishes like noodles, kimchi, meat, soups, noodles, and desserts. There are many dishes in these books that you can cook easily. These dishes will add flavor to your next party, so get ready to pen down the names of these cookbooks.

The appropriate number of calories and nutrients from Korean recipes must be consumed to sustain overall weight. A person's general well-being and health depend on appropriate eating, working out, and maintaining a balanced weight. Since we know you're anxious to see what we have in store for you, we won't take any more of your time. We hope that you enjoy this cookbook and conquer the recipes to come.

# Chapter 3
# Basic Stocks, Sauces, and Marinades

## Beef Stock
**Prep time: 5 minutes | Cook time: 2 hours 10 minutes | Serves 4**

- 2 pounds beef brisket, rinsed
- 8 quarts water, or enough to fill a large stockpot

1. In a large stockpot over high heat, bring the beef and water to a boil.
2. Reduce the heat to low and simmer, uncovered, for at least 2 hours until fork-tender, skimming the top occasionally to remove the foam and fat.
3. Transfer the brisket to a cutting board. You can slice it, shred it, and use it immediately or reserve it for later use.
4. Use the broth immediately, or for later use, store it in the refrigerator for up to 1 week or in the freezer for up to 2 months.

## Sensational Soy Dipping Sauce
**Prep time: 5 minutes | Cook time: 0 | Serves 4**

- ⅓ cup soy sauce
- ⅓ cup rice wine vinegar
- 1 tablespoon toasted sesame oil
- 1 tablespoon gochugara
- 1 tablespoon thinly sliced scallions
- 1 teaspoon minced garlic

1. In a medium bowl, whisk together all of the ingredients.
2. Transfer to an air-tight glass container and store in the refrigerator for up to 2 weeks.

## Chojang (Vinegar Gochujang Sauce)
**Prep time: 5 minutes | Cook time: 10 minutes | Makes about ½ cup**

- ¼ cup gochujang
- ¼ cup rice vinegar
- 2 tablespoons sugar
- 2 tablespoons pineapple juice (substituting orange juice is OK)

1. Combine gochujang, vinegar, sugar and pineapple juice in a bowl and whisk together until fully combined. The texture should be smooth with no chunks of gochujang remaining.
2. Leftover sauce keeps for up to 1 week, refrigerated.

## Sweet and Spicy Dipping Sauce
**Prep time: 5 minutes | Cook time: 0 | Serves 4**

- 5 tablespoons gochujang
- 1 tablespoon sugar
- 2 tablespoons honey
- 3 tablespoons rice wine vinegar
- 2 teaspoons minced garlic
- 1 teaspoon toasted sesame oil

1. In a medium bowl, whisk all of the ingredients together until well blended.
2. If the sauce is too thick, add 1 to 2 teaspoons of warm water to thin it out.
3. Use immediately or store in an airtight glass container in the refrigerator for up to 2 weeks.

## Seasoned Soy Sauce
**Prep time: 5 minutes | Cook time: 0 | Serves 4**

- 4 tablespoons soy sauce
- 1 scallion, finely chopped
- 1 garlic clove, minced
- 1 tablespoon toasted sesame oil
- 1 tablespoon toasted sesame seeds
- ½ tablespoon gochugaru
- ½ teaspoon freshly ground black pepper (optional)

1. In a small bowl, whisk together all of the ingredients to combine well.
2. Transfer to an airtight glass container and store in the refrigerator for up to 1 week.

## Vegetable Dipping Sauce
**Prep time: 5 minutes | Cook time: 5 minutes | Serves 8 as a condiment**

- ¼ cup fermented bean paste
- 2 tablespoons Korean chili paste
- 2 tablespoons sesame oil
- 1 tablespoon honey
- 2 teaspoons sesame seeds
- 1 garlic clove, minced
- ½ small yellow onion, diced

1. Combine all ingredients in a medium bowl and mix well. Serve at room temperature. Refrigerate in an airtight container for up to 2 weeks.

## Korean Chili Sauce

**Prep time: 5 minutes | Cook time: 5 minutes | Serves 4**

- ½ cup Korean chili paste
- 1 garlic clove, minced
- 2 teaspoons sesame oil
- 1 tablespoon honey
- 1 tablespoon maple syrup
- 1 tablespoon apple cider vinegar
- 2 tablespoons water
- 1 tablespoon white sesame seeds

1. Combine all ingredients in a medium bowl and mix well. Refrigerate in an airtight container for up to 2 weeks.

## Green Onion and Vinegar Sauce

**Prep time: 10 minutes | Makes 1 cup**

- 2 green onions, finely chopped
- ¼ cup rice vinegar
- 1 tablespoon toasted sesame oil
- 1 teaspoon white sugar
- ½ teaspoon kosher salt
- ½ teaspoon sesame seeds

1. In a small bowl, thoroughly combine the green onions, vinegar, oil, sugar, salt, and sesame seeds. Serve the sauce at room temperature.

# Chapter 4
# Kimchi

## Napa Cabbage Kimchi

**Prep time:** 30 minutes, plus 6 hours to marinate and 48 hours to ferment | **Cook time:** 0 | **Serves** 12

- 1 cup coarse sea salt
- 10 cups water
- 2 heads napa cabbage, cut into 2-inch squares
- 1 tablespoon finely chopped garlic
- 1 tablespoon chopped ginger
- ½ cup gochugaru
- 2 tablespoons sugar
- 5 scallions, cut into ½-inch pieces
- 2 tablespoons fish sauce

1. In a very large nonreactive (such as glass, ceramic, or plastic) bowl or pot, stir the salt into the water until mixed.
2. Add the cabbage to the salt water and, if necessary, weigh down with large plate so all of the leaves are completely submerged. Marinate the cabbage for 5 to 6 hours.
3. Remove the cabbage, discarding the marinating liquid, and rinse it in cold water. Squeeze out any excess liquid.
4. In a very large bowl, mix the garlic, ginger, gochugaru, sugar, scallions, and fish sauce. Add the cabbage to the bowl and toss to coat with the seasoning mixture.
5. Pack the seasoned cabbage into a large, airtight jar. Leave at least 4 to 5 inches at the top to allow for expansion during the fermentation process.
6. Let the kimchi ferment in a cool, dark place (such as a shady corner or countertop) for 2 to 3 days before serving or refrigerating.
7. Store in the refrigerator in an airtight container for up to 6 months.

## Cubed Radish Kimchi

**Prep time:** 30 minutes, plus 2 hours to marinate and 24 hours to ferment | **Cook time:** 0 | **Serves** 8

- 3½ pounds Korean radish, peeled and cut into ¾-inch cubes
- 2 cups sea salt, plus 1 tablespoon
- 5 teaspoons sugar
- 6 tablespoons gochugaru
- ½ large onion, finely chopped
- 2 garlic cloves, minced
- 1 teaspoon fish sauce
- 2 scallions, chopped
- 1-inch piece fresh ginger, peeled and finely chopped

1. Put the radish in a large bowl and cover with 2 cups salt. Mix gently to combine. Let sit at room temperature for 2 hours. Any water will drain away, collecting at the bottom of the bowl.
2. Rinse the radish well with cold water and drain thoroughly.
3. In a large bowl, combine the sugar, gochugaru, onion, garlic, fish sauce, scallions, ginger, and the remaining 1 tablespoon salt and mix well. Add the radish and toss to coat.
4. Transfer the seasoned radish into an airtight glass container (leaving 2 inches at the top), cover, and store at room temperature for at least 24 hours.
5. Serve immediately, or store in an airtight glass container in the refrigerator for up to 2 months.

**The Korean Home Kitchen** | 13

## Stuffed Cucumber Kimchi

**Prep time: 30 minutes, plus 30 minutes to marinate and 8 to 12 hours to ferment | Cook time: 0 | Serves 12**

- 10 Korean, pickling, or kirby cucumbers, with the ends trimmed
- ¼ cup sea salt
- 4 garlic cloves, minced
- ½ cup gochugaru
- ½ cup Asian chives, cut into 1-inch pieces
- ⅓ cup fish sauce
- ⅓ cup shredded carrots
- 2 tablespoons sugar

1. Stand one cucumber up on its end on the cutting board and slice down the middle vertically without cutting all the way through the end. Rotate the cucumber and make another vertical cut without going through the end, so that the second cut is perpendicular to the first. Repeat for the remaining 9 cucumbers.
2. Fill a large bowl with water and add the salt. Stir to dissolve. Add the cut cucumbers in this salt bath and keep them submerged for 30 minutes. If necessary, weight them down with a plate so they remain covered with the salt bath.
3. While the cucumbers are marinating, mix the garlic, gochugaru, chives, fish sauce, carrots, and sugar together in a large bowl.
4. When the cucumbers have marinated for 30 minutes, remove them from the salt bath. Do not rinse them. Stuff the seasoning mixture into each cucumber, filling the spaces between the connected spears. Do not rinse out the large bowl that held the seasoning mixture. Lay cucumbers down next to each other in an airtight glass container.
5. Fill the seasoning bowl with 1 cup of water, stirring to mix it with the remaining seasoning in the bowl. Pour this mixture over the cucumbers in the containers until they are almost submerged.
6. Cover with a tight-fitting lid and store at room temperature for 8 to 12 hours. Serve immediately or store in the refrigerator for up to 1 month.

## Tomato Kimchi

**Prep time: 5 minutes | Cook time: 35 minutes | Serves 4 (as banchan)**

- 1 pint grape tomatoes, halved lengthwise
- 1 garlic clove, minced
- 1 scallion, trimmed and sliced into thin, wispy ribbons (white and light green parts)
- ½ teaspoon peeled, minced ginger
- ½ teaspoon kosher salt
- 1 teaspoon Korean chili flake
- ½ teaspoon fish sauce
- 2 teaspoons maple syrup

1. Combine all ingredients except the tomatoes in a mixing bowl and whisk to combine.
2. Add tomatoes and toss until they're well-coated in the marinade. Serve immediately, or store for 1 to 2 days in the fridge.

## Scallion Kimchi

**Prep time: 20 minutes, plus 30 minutes to marinate and 24 hours to ferment | Cook time: 10 minutes | Serves 8**

- 2 pounds scallions, trimmed
- ⅓ cup fish sauce
- 1 cup water
- 2 tablespoons sweet rice flour
- 2 Asian pears, peeled, cored, and puréed
- 4 garlic cloves, puréed
- 1-inch piece fresh ginger, peeled and puréed
- 2 cups gochugaru
- 2 tablespoons toasted sesame seeds
- 1½ tablespoons sugar
- 1 teaspoon rice wine vinegar

1. Dry the scallions well with paper towels. In a large mixing bowl, add the scallions, pour the fish sauce over them, and toss to coat well. Let sit at room temperature for 20 to 30 minutes.
2. While the scallions are marinating, prepare the sauce. In a small saucepan over medium heat, combine the water and sweet rice flour, stirring gently. Heat until bubbly. Remove from the heat and let cool.
3. While the flour mixture is cooling, make a seasoning paste. In a large mixing bowl, mix together the puréed pears, garlic, and ginger. Add the gochugaru, sesame seeds, sugar, and vinegar and mix well.
4. When the flour mixture has cooled, mix it thoroughly into the bowl with the seasoning paste. Pour the seasoning mixture over the scallions and fish sauce. Mix gently and thoroughly.
5. Place the scallions into an airtight glass jar, arranging them neatly. Pour the remaining sauce over the top. Screw on the lid loosely and let sit at room temperature for 1 day and up to 2 days.
6. Store in the refrigerator for up to 1 month.

## Sliced Radish and Cabbage Water Kimchi

**Prep time:** 10 minutes, plus 1 hour to marinate and 24 hours to ferment | **Cook time:** 10 minutes | **Makes** 1 gallon (3.8 L)

- 2 ½ pounds (1.2 kg) moo radish, scrubbed and peeled
- 1 ½ pounds (680 g/about ½ large) napa cabbage, cored
- ¼ cup (60 g) kosher salt
- 3 tablespoons coarse sea salt
- 1 bunch scallions, white parts only, cut into 2-inch (5 cm) pieces
- 1 Holland chile, halved lengthwise
- 8 cloves garlic, minced
- 2-inch (5 cm) piece peeled fresh ginger, julienned
- 2 tablespoons gochugaru
- 1 tablespoon granulated sugar

1. Cut the radishes in half lengthwise. Then cut each half into thirds, lengthwise, then cut the thirds into ¼-inch (6 mm) slices. Set aside in a large mixing bowl.
2. Cut the cabbage in half lengthwise, then into 2-inch (5 cm) slices, and add them to the bowl with the radishes.
3. Toss 2 tablespoons of the kosher salt and the sea salt together with the vegetables and let them sit, loosely covered, for 3 hours at room temperature. Discard any water that accumulates in the bottom of the bowl and transfer the vegetables to a clean, large bowl, plastic storage container, or glass gallon jar with the scallions, chile, garlic, and ginger and set it aside.
4. Put the gochugaru in a cheesecloth bundle or tea ball, and add it to a large mixing bowl, stockpot, or glass gallon jar with 12 cups (3 L) water. After the gochugaru just begins to color the water red, about 5 minutes, remove the gochugaru, squeezing out the liquid (if it is in the cheesecloth) into the pot.
5. Dissolve the sugar and remaining 2 tablespoons kosher salt in the water, then pour the water mixture over the vegetables.
6. Stir it together and let it sit, loosely covered, at room temperature for 1 hour. Taste for seasoning, and add more salt and sugar as desired.
7. Let the vegetables sit, loosely covered, at room temperature for 24 hours, then move it to the refrigerator. It will keep for 2 months.

## Garlic Chive Kimch

**Prep time:** 30 minutes, plus 2 hours to marinate and 48 hours to ferment | **Cook time:** 5 minutes | **Makes** 8 cups (2 L)

- 2 bunches garlic chives
- 2 tablespoons kosher salt
- 2 Holland chiles, seeded and thinly sliced
- 2 Korean green chiles, seeded and thinly sliced
- 1 cup (120 g) gochugaru
- ⅓ cup (75 ml) fish sauce
- 2 tablespoons minced garlic

1. Trim the root ends of the garlic chives, but keep them whole. Gently wash the garlic chives under running water, then rinse and drain them.
2. In a mixing bowl, toss the chives with the salt and let them sit for 1 hour, then drain off any liquid and rinse the chives under running water.
3. Combine the remaining ingredients in a mixing bowl with the rinsed chives and ½ cup (120 ml) water, making sure the chives are coated with the marinade.
4. Let the chives sit, covered, in the refrigerator for 2 days before serving. They will keep in the refrigerator for 3 to 4 weeks.

## Whole Radish Water Kimchi

**Prep time:** 30 minutes, plus 2 hours to marinate and 24 hours to ferment | **Cook time:** 15 minutes | **Makes** 1 gallon (3.8 L)

- 3 pounds (1.4 kg) moo radish
- ⅓ cup (40 g) kosher salt
- 2 scallions, blanched in boiling water
- 1 Asian pear, peeled, cored, and cut into quarters
- 5 cloves garlic, crushed
- 1-inch (2.5 cm) piece peeled fresh ginger, cut into three pieces
- 1 Korean green chile, halved lengthwise, seeds and membrane removed

1. Clean the radishes well by scrubbing them under running water. Let them dry completely.
2. Working in a mixing bowl, rub the salt all over the radishes.
3. Put the salted radish in a large nonreactive container and let sit, loosely covered, at room temperature for 4 to 5 days. (A large glass jar with a screw top is ideal.)
4. Add the remaining ingredients to the jar and cover with 12 cups (2.8 L) cold water.
5. Give the mixture a stir and taste the broth: It should taste like seasoned water, so add more salt if needed.
6. Let the jar sit at room temperature, loosely covered, for 24 hours, then keep it in the refrigerator for at least 2 and preferably 3 weeks before serving.
7. To serve the dongchimi, remove the radishes from the liquid and cut them into slices, or use the liquid in soups and stews. It will keep in the refrigerator for 3 months.

The Korean Home Kitchen | 15

## Perilla Kimchi

**Prep time:** 30 minutes, plus 2 hours to marinate and 24 hours to ferment | **Cook time:** 5 minutes | **Serves 8 to 10**

- 2 ounces (55 g) perilla or shiso leaves (about 50 leaves)
- 3 tablespoons fish sauce
- 2 tablespoons honey
- ¼ cup (60 ml) soy sauce
- ⅓ cup (40 g) gochugaru
- 1 medium white onion, thinly sliced
- 3 tablespoons minced garlic
- 2 tablespoons minced peeled fresh ginger
- 1 small carrot, grated or julienned
- 1 Holland chile, halved lengthwise, seeds removed, and thinly sliced
- 1 tablespoon toasted sesame seeds

1. Wash the perilla leaves thoroughly and let them dry completely.
2. In a medium bowl, combine the remaining ingredients to make the seasoning paste.
3. Make a stack of 2 to 3 perilla leaves, then spread 1 to 2 teaspoons of the seasoning on top of the stack. Place the stacks on top of each other in a glass or plastic airtight container and store them in the fridge. The leaves will keep for several weeks in the refrigerator.

## Salted Preserved Squid In Spicy Sauce

**Prep time:** 30 minutes, plus 1 hour to marinate | **Cook time:** 15 minutes | **Makes 12 ounces (340 g)**

- 1 pound (455 g) fresh squid, cleaned
- ¼ cup (60 g) kosher salt
- ⅔ cup (165 ml) gochugaru
- ⅓ cup (75 ml) brown rice syrup
- 1 tablespoon fish sauce
- 10 cloves garlic, thinly sliced
- 2 Holland chiles, thinly sliced
- 2 Korean long green chiles, thinly sliced
- Toasted sesame seeds
- Sesame oil, for drizzling

1. Rinse the squid under cold running water and pat dry. Separate the tentacles from the bodies, and if the tentacles are really large, cut them in half (you want to be able to pick them up with chopsticks and eat them).
2. Place the squid in a nonreactive baking dish and rub the salt into the bodies and the tentacles. Let sit, at room temperature, for 1 hour, then refrigerate overnight.
3. The next day, rinse all the salt off the squid and let it drain well in a colander set over a bowl or the sink. Pat the squid dry and cut the bodies into thin strips.
4. In a small mixing bowl, combine the gochugaru, brown rice syrup, fish sauce, garlic, chiles, and sesame seeds. Taste for seasoning and add more salt, fish sauce, or brown rice syrup as needed.
5. Add the squid to the bowl and mix well, ensuring the pieces are fully coated, then pack them into a glass jar and store in the refrigerator.
6. You can eat this right away, drizzled with some sesame oil, though the flavors will continue to develop over time. It lasts in the refrigerator for about 3 weeks.

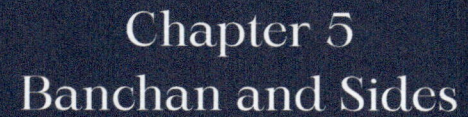

# Chapter 5
# Banchan and Sides

## Steamed Eggs

**Prep time: 5 minutes | Cook time: 25 minutes | Serves 4**

- 1½ cups Korean stock or water
- 5 large eggs, beaten
- 1 tablespoon saeujeot (salted fermented shrimp) or fish sauce, or 2 teaspoons coarse sea salt
- 1 scallion, both white and green parts, chopped

1. Pour 1 cup of water into the Instant Pot. Place a trivet inside.
2. In a 4-quart, oven-safe bowl or earthen pot that fits in the Instant Pot, mix together the stock and eggs.
3. Add the saeujeot, and mix well.
4. Sprinkle the scallion on top. Place a piece of aluminum foil over the bowl, and carefully place the bowl on the trivet in the Instant Pot. Lock the lid, and close the steam valve. Set the timer for 4 minutes on High Pressure.
5. When the timer sounds, natural release the steam for 6 minutes, then quick release the remainder. Open the lid. Serve immediately.

## Seasoned Rice Balls

**Prep time: 15 minutes | Cook time: 30 minutes | Serves 6**

- 2 cups short-grain rice
- ½ teaspoon coarse sea salt
- 1 tablespoon sesame oil
- 2 tablespoons rice seasoning mix (furikake)
- Kimchi or pickled vegetables, for serving (optional)

1. Rinse the rice under cold water, and drain. Repeat this process until the water turns clear. Drain the rice at the final rinse, and put it directly in the Instant Pot.
2. Add 1¾ cups of water, lock the lid, and close the steam valve. Set the timer for 2 minutes on High Pressure.
3. When the timer sounds, natural release the steam for 10 minutes, then quick release the remainder. (It is very important that you quick release immediately after 10 minutes.) Open the lid.
4. Add the salt, oil, and rice seasoning mix. Mix well. Let the rice cool for about 3 minutes, or until cool enough to touch.
5. Using a spoon, scoop out about 2 tablespoons of the rice onto the palms of your hands. Roll it into a ball. Serve the rice balls with kimchi (if using).

## Braised Lotus Root

**Prep time: 5 minutes | Cook time: 40 minutes | Serves 6**

- 1 pound lotus root
- 1 tablespoon rice vinegar
- 5 tablespoons soy sauce
- 4 teaspoons rice wine
- 2 teaspoons granulated white sugar
- 2 teaspoons sesame oil, divided
- 3 tablespoons corn syrup or 2 tablespoons honey
- 1 tablespoon sesame seeds (optional)

1. Using a potato peeler, peel the skin off the lotus root, and cut off the tough ends. Cut it into ¼-inch-thick rounds. Put them directly into the Instant Pot.
2. Add the vinegar and enough water to cover the lotus. Lock the lid, and close the steam valve. Set the timer for 3 minutes on High Pressure.
3. When the timer sounds, natural release the steam for 5 minutes, then quick release the remainder. Open the lid.
4. Drain the lotus root, and rinse in cold water.
5. Return the lotus root to the Instant Pot, and add 1 cup of water, the soy sauce, rice wine, sugar, and 1 teaspoon of oil. Lock the lid, and close the steam valve. Set the timer for 1 minute on High Pressure.
6. When the timer sounds, natural release the steam for 5 minutes, then quick release the remainder.
7. Open the lid. Press the Sauté button, and set to High.
8. Once the screen reads HOT, add the remaining 1 teaspoon of oil and the corn syrup. Stir well, and allow the mixture to come to a boil, being mindful not to burn the sauce, about 5 minutes. Turn off the Instant Pot.
9. Sprinkle with sesame seeds for garnish before serving (if using).

## Braised Potatoes

**Prep time:** 15 minutes | **Cook time:** 55 minutes | **Serves 4**

- 1 pound baby potatoes
- 2 tablespoons vegetable oil
- ½ cup soy sauce
- 2 tablespoons light brown sugar
- 1 yellow onion
- 2 green chile peppers or ½ green bell pepper, seeded and chopped (optional)
- 2 garlic cloves, minced
- 1 tablespoon rice syrup
- 2 tablespoons sesame oil
- 1 teaspoon black pepper
- 2 scallions, both white and green parts, chopped
- 1 tablespoon sesame seeds

1. Wash the potatoes in cold water. Press the Sauté button, and set to High.
2. Once the screen reads HOT, pour the vegetable oil into the Instant Pot. Add the potatoes, and sauté for 5 minutes, or until the potatoes are slightly seared on all sides. Turn off the Sauté mode.
3. Add 1 cup of water, the soy sauce, and sugar. Lock the lid, and close the steam valve. Set the timer for 15 minutes on High Pressure.
4. When the timer sounds, natural release the steam for 10 minutes, then quick release the remainder. Open the lid.
5. Add the onion, chile peppers (if using), garlic, rice syrup, sesame oil, and pepper.
6. Press the Sauté button, and set to High. Let the mixture come to a boil. Cook for about 5 minutes, or until the sauce is reduced and the onions are soft.
7. Turn off the Instant Pot. Add the scallions and sesame seeds before serving.

## Steamed Eggplant

**Prep time:** 15 minutes | **Cook time:** 25 minutes | **Serves 4**

- 2 medium Korean or Japanese eggplants (about 8 ounces total)
- 1 garlic clove, minced
- 1 scallion, both white and green parts, chopped
- 2 tablespoons soy sauce
- 1 teaspoon sesame oil
- 1 teaspoon gochugaru (Korean red chili flakes)
- 1 teaspoon sesame seeds
- ½ teaspoon minced fresh ginger
- ½ teaspoon granulated white sugar
- ¼ teaspoon black pepper

1. Cut the stems off the eggplants, but otherwise leave them whole.
2. Pour 1 cup of water into the Instant Pot, and drop in a steamer basket.
3. Put the eggplants in the steamer basket, lock the lid, and close the steam valve. Set the timer for 1 minute on High Pressure.
4. When the timer sounds, quick release the steam. Open the lid. Immediately take out the eggplants, place them on a plate, and let them cool to the touch, 5 minutes.
5. Once cool enough, quarter the eggplants lengthwise, then cut crosswise and into 4 equal parts. Transfer to a bowl.
6. To make the sauce, in a separate small bowl, combine the garlic, scallion, soy sauce, oil, gochugaru, sesame seeds, ginger, sugar, and pepper. Mix well.
7. Pour the sauce over the eggplant. Gently distribute the sauce throughout the eggplant, and serve immediately.

## Stir-Fried Fish Cake

**Prep time: 5 minutes | Cook time: 15 minutes | Serves 4**

- 2 sheets (½ package or 1 pound) frozen fish cakes, thawed
- 1 tablespoon soy sauce
- 1 tablespoon rice vinegar
- 1 tablespoon toasted sesame oil
- 2 teaspoons white sugar
- 1 teaspoon garlic powder
- 1 teaspoon kosher salt
- 1 teaspoon coarse ground black pepper
- 1 tablespoon vegetable oil
- ½ small yellow onion, thinly sliced

1. Cut the fish cake sheets into 1-by-2-inch rectangles, and set aside.
2. In a small bowl, mix together the soy sauce, vinegar, sesame oil, sugar, garlic powder, salt, and pepper to make the sauce.
3. In a medium pan, heat the vegetable oil over medium-high heat. Sauté the onion for 5 minutes, until it softens. Add the thawed fish cakes and stir for 3 minutes more, until they start to soften up. Add the sauce and stir until evenly incorporated. Turn off the heat and let it rest for 2 minutes.
4. Spoon the eomuk bokkeum into a small serving bowl and serve at room temperature.

## Seasoned Spinach

**Prep time: 5 minutes | Cook time: 15 minutes | Serves 4**

- 2 cups ice
- 2 cups water
- 1 pound spinach
- 1 teaspoon minced garlic
- 1 tablespoon soy sauce
- 1 tablespoon toasted sesame oil
- 1 teaspoon kosher salt
- 1 teaspoon sesame seeds

1. In a large bowl, combine the ice and water. Set aside.
2. Bring a medium pot of water to a boil over high heat. Add the spinach and cook for 2 minutes, until wilted. Then, using a spider or slotted spoon, immediately transfer the spinach to the ice bath. Let cool for about 30 seconds.
3. Once the spinach is cool, transfer it to a kitchen towel and wring out as much water as possible.
4. In a small bowl, toss the spinach with the garlic, soy sauce, oil, salt, and sesame seeds until incorporated.
5. Place the sigeumchi namul on a small platter and serve.

## Spicy Cucumber Salad

**Prep time: 15 minutes, plus 1 hour to dry brine the cucumbers | Cook time: 5 minutes | Serves 4**

- 5 Korean cucumbers, cut into ¼-inch slices
- 1 tablespoon kosher salt, for dry brining
- 1 small white onion, thinly sliced
- 1 Fresno chile, seeded and coarsely chopped
- 1 medium carrot, julienned
- 2 tablespoons minced garlic
- 2 tablespoons coarse gochugaru flakes
- 2 tablespoons toasted sesame oil
- 2 tablespoons rice vinegar
- 1 tablespoon fish sauce
- 2 teaspoons lightly packed dark brown sugar
- ½ teaspoon sesame seeds

1. In a strainer, toss the cucumber pieces in the salt. Place the strainer in a bowl to catch the excess water being pulled out. Set aside for 1 hour.
2. Rinse the salt off the cucumber pieces and pat dry with a paper towel. Discard any liquid that was drawn out of the cucumbers.
3. In a large mixing bowl, combine the cucumber pieces with the onion, chile, carrot, garlic, gochugaru, oil, vinegar, fish sauce, and brown sugar. Mix well, evenly coating the vegetables.
4. Garnish the salad with sesame seeds and serve in a small bowl.

## Korean Lettuce Salad
**Prep time: 15 minutes | Cook time: 5 minutes | Serves 4**

- For the dressing
- 1 tablespoon rice vinegar
- 1 tablespoon toasted sesame oil
- 1 teaspoon coarse gochugaru flakes
- 1 teaspoon garlic powder
- 1 teaspoon coarse ground black pepper
- 1 teaspoon kosher salt
- For the salad
- 1 head red leaf lettuce, coarsely chopped into 1-inch pieces
- 1 small yellow onion, thinly sliced

1. To make the dressing: In a small bowl, whisk together the vinegar, oil, gochugaru, garlic powder, pepper, and salt.
2. To make the salad: Just before serving, in a serving bowl, combine the lettuce, onion, and dressing. Toss the salad to evenly incorporate the dressing and serve.

## Spicy Braised Tofu

**Prep time: 15 minutes | Cook time: 20 minutes | Serves 4**

- 1 (14-ounce) package firm tofu, drained (not pressed)
- 2 tablespoons vegetable oil
- 3 tablespoons soy sauce
- 1 tablespoon minced garlic
- 1 tablespoon coarse gochugaru flakes
- 1 tablespoon lightly packed dark brown sugar
- 1 tablespoon rice vinegar
- 1 tablespoon toasted sesame oil
- ½ cup water
- ¼ teaspoon sesame seeds
- 2 green onions, thinly sliced, for garnish

1. Halve the tofu block lengthwise, then cut it into ½-inch-thick squares. Pat dry with a paper towel.
2. In a large nonstick pan, heat the vegetable oil over medium-high heat. Fry the tofu pieces for about 5 minutes per side, until they're browned on each side.
3. In a small bowl, whisk together the soy sauce, garlic, gochugaru, brown sugar, vinegar, sesame oil, and water.
4. Increase the heat under the tofu to high and add the braising sauce. Bring it to a boil, then reduce the heat to medium-low and cover the pan. Simmer for about 10 minutes, occasionally flipping the tofu pieces, until the braising liquid reduces to a syrup and the tofu pieces are coated. Remove the pan from the heat.
5. Transfer the dubu jorim to a medium serving platter and sprinkle with sesame seeds and green onions to serve.

# Chapter 6
# The Main Event

## Classic Korean Beef
**Prep time: 10 minutes | Cook time: 25 minutes | Serves 4 TO 6**

- 1 large Korean pear, peeled
- 6 tbsp (90 ml) soy sauce
- 1 tbsp (15 ml) Korean tuna sauce or Korean soy sauce for soup
- 2 tbsp (26 g) sugar
- ¼ cup (60 ml) Korean oligo syrup or corn syrup
- 3 cloves garlic, finely minced
- ½ tsp freshly ground black pepper
- 1 cup (240 ml) water
- 21 oz (600 g) very thinly sliced beef sirloin, thawed if frozen
- 1 medium onion, sliced
- 5 oz (140 g) enoki or sliced button mushrooms
- 10 oz (280 g) bok choy, quartered (optional)
- 2 green onions, thinly sliced diagonally
- 2 tsp (10 ml) sesame oil
- Cooked rice, for serving

1. Put a large fine-mesh strainer or sieve over a large bowl. Grate the pear on a fine cheese grater over the strainer to catch all the pulp. Grate until you reach the core of the pear. Discard the seeds.
2. Using the back of a wooden spoon, press the grated pear pulp firmly through the strainer to collect the fresh pear juice. You will get about 1 cup (240 ml) of juice. Discard any pulp that remains in the strainer.
3. Add the soy sauce, tuna sauce, sugar, syrup, garlic, pepper and water to the pear juice and mix well until the sugar dissolves, 30 to 60 seconds. Add the beef, separating each slice, and the onion to the mixture, then toss with your hands to help the meat soak up the marinade. Let it sit on the counter for 20 minutes.
4. Heat a large, deep skillet over medium-high heat until hot. Add the beef, onion and the marinade along with the mushrooms and bok choy, if using. Gently stir everything in the skillet and cook until the beef is browned, 2 to 3 minutes.
5. Add the green onions and drizzle the sesame oil on the beef; toss gently. Serve immediately with rice. Don't forget to drizzle some of the broth over your rice to soak up that wonderful flavor. Any kind of kimchi would be a nice accompaniment.

## Southern-Style Beef Rib Patties

**Prep time: 5 minutes | Cook time: 15 minutes | Makes 6 to 8 patties**

- PATTIES
- 17.5 oz (500 g) beef rib meat or sirloin, or combination of both, diced
- ½ medium onion, finely minced
- 1 Asian leek, white part only, finely minced
- ¼ cup (36 g) sweet rice flour
- 3 cloves garlic, finely minced
- ¼ cup (35 g) finely chopped pine nuts or walnuts, plus more for garnish (optional)
- 2 tbsp (30 ml) soy sauce
- ½ tsp salt
- ¾ tsp freshly ground black pepper
- 1 tbsp (15 g) light brown sugar
- 2 tsp (10 ml) sesame oil
- 2 tbsp (30 ml) cooking oil
- Alfalfa sprouts, for garnish (optional)
- HONEY GLAZE
- 3 tbsp (63 g) honey
- 2 tbsp (30 ml) soy sauce
- 1 tbsp (15 ml) sesame oil
- Cooked rice, for serving

1. To prepare the patties, place the diced beef in a food processor and pulse a few times until you get small but coarse pieces slightly larger than ground beef. It is okay to have a few pieces that are bigger than the others.
2. Transfer the beef to the bowl of an electric mixer and add all the patty ingredients, except the cooking oil and garnishes, and stir briefly with a wooden spoon to combine. Then, using the paddle attachment, mix at high speed for 2 minutes, or until the mixture becomes very sticky and all the ingredients are well incorporated.
3. Divide the meat mixture into 6 to 8 portions (or any other size you desire) and shape it into patties. Set aside.
4. In a large skillet, heat 1 tablespoon (15 ml) of the cooking oil over medium heat. Place the patties in the skillet and cook until they're browned, 2 to 3 minutes. Flip them to the other side and continue to cook for another 2 minutes, or until completely cooked, adding a little more oil if needed and adjusting the heat so the patties do not burn.
5. Meanwhile, prepare the glaze. In a small bowl, combine the honey, soy sauce and sesame oil. Drizzle the glaze over the beef while it's still in the skillet and let it sizzle for 10 seconds.
6. Transfer the patties to a serving plate and garnish with alfalfa sprouts or pine nuts, if desired. Serve hot with rice.

### Pork Ribs With Garlic, Pear & Jujube

**Prep time: 5 minutes | Cook time: 15 minutes | Serves 4**

2½ lb (1.1 kg) pork short ribs
1 large Korean pear, peeled, seeded and diced
½ large onion, diced
¼ cup (60 ml) soy sauce
3 tbsp (45 ml) sweet rice wine (mirin)
1 tsp pureed fresh ginger
2 tbsp (30 ml) Korean plum extract or corn syrup
½ tsp freshly ground black pepper
2 tbsp (30 ml) cooking oil
8 to 10 cloves garlic, thinly sliced
5 or 6 dried jujubes
2 tbsp (13 g) thinly sliced fresh ginger, for garnish
1 green onion, finely chopped, for garnish
1 tbsp (8 g) toasted sesame seeds, for garnish
Cooked rice, for serving

1. Put the pork ribs into a large pot and pour in enough water to cover them. Bring the water to a boil over high heat and cook, uncovered, for 3 to 4 minutes. Remove the ribs from the pot and rinse them with hot water; set aside. Discard the cooking liquid.
2. In a blender, puree the pear and onion until smooth, adding a little water, if needed, to help the blade run. Place a fine sieve over a large bowl and pour the pear puree into the sieve. Press down with the back of a wooden spoon to collect the juice. Discard the fibrous pulp remaining in the sieve. You should be able to collect about 1½ cups (360 ml) of juice.
3. Add the soy sauce, rice wine, ginger puree, plum extract and pepper to the pear juice to make a sauce; stir well and set aside.
4. In a large, deep, lidded skillet or wok, heat the oil over medium-low heat, add the garlic slices and fry them until they turn light golden brown and crisp, 2 to 3 minutes, being careful not to burn them, adjusting the heat level, if needed. Remove the skillet from the heat and, leaving the garlic-infused oil in the pan, transfer the fried garlic slices to a paper towel-lined plate; set aside.
5. Return the skillet to medium-high heat and add the pork ribs; stir-fry them for 1 minute. Add the sauce and the dried jujubes to the skillet; mix well and let the mixture come to a boil. Lower the heat to medium-low and simmer, covered, for 20 minutes.
6. Uncover the skillet and increase the heat to high. Bring the sauce to a boil again and let it thicken until it attains a very thick, glazelike consistency, tossing the ribs occasionally, about 5 minutes.
7. Put the glazed ribs on a serving platter and garnish with the sliced ginger, green onion, sesame seeds and fried garlic slices. Serve hot with rice.

## Spicy Pork Stir-Fry
**Prep time: 5 minutes | Cook time: 10 minutes | Serves 4**

- 21 oz (600 g) thinly sliced pork shoulder or pork butt
- 1 tbsp (15 ml) soy sauce
- ¼ cup (66 g) Korean chili paste
- 1 to 2 tbsp (6 to 12 g) Korean chili flakes
- 2 to 3 tbsp (42 to 63 g) honey
- 1 tbsp (10 g) minced garlic
- 1 tsp pureed fresh ginger
- 2 tbsp (30 ml) sweet rice wine (mirin)
- 1 tbsp (15 ml) sesame oil
- Freshly ground black pepper
- 1 tbsp (15 ml) cooking oil
- 1 medium onion, sliced
- 1 fresh green chile, sliced (optional)
- 1 green onion, sliced
- Sesame seeds
- Cooked rice, for serving
- Lettuce leaves, for serving

1. Make sure to drain away any liquid coming out of the pork if you thaw it from frozen. Place the pork in a large bowl.
2. In a small bowl, combine the soy sauce, chili paste, chili flakes, honey, garlic, ginger, rice wine, sesame oil and black pepper; mix well.
3. Pour the sauce over the pork and mix it together with your hands as if you are massaging the pork, to ensure the sauce infuses every piece of pork.
4. In a large, heavy-bottomed skillet, heat the cooking oil over medium-high heat until it's very hot. Cooking in batches, if necessary, add the pork, onion and chile, if using, to the skillet. You should hear the loud sizzling sound immediately. Do not overcrowd the skillet. Stir-fry the pork and onion until they are fully cooked, 3 to 4 minutes.
5. Sprinkle the green onion and sesame seeds on top. Serve hot with rice and lettuce to wrap the pork.

## Korean Sweet & Sour Pork

**Prep time: 5 minutes | Cook time: 20 minutes | Serves 6**

- 1 lb (455 g) pork loin, sliced into ½" (1.3-cm)-thick strips
- 1 tbsp (15 ml) sweet rice wine (mirin)
- ½ tsp salt
- ½ tsp pureed fresh ginger
- ½ tsp freshly ground black pepper
- BATTER
- ¾ cup (96 g) potato starch
- ¼ cup (32 g) cornstarch
- ½ cup (120 ml) + 1 to 2 tbsp (15 to 30 ml) water
- 2 tbsp (30 ml) cooking oil
- Peanut oil, for deep-frying
- SAUCE
- 1½ cups (360 ml) + 3 tbsp (45 ml) water, divided
- 7 tbsp (91 g) sugar
- 1 tbsp (15 ml) soy sauce
- ¼ cup (60 ml) white vinegar
- ¼ tsp salt
- 3 tbsp (24 g) potato starch
- ½ medium onion, diced
- ½ red bell pepper, diced
- 1.5 oz (45 g) fresh wood ear mushrooms (optional)
- ½ English cucumber, diced

1. In a bowl, combine the pork, rice wine, salt, ginger and black pepper; toss well and set it aside for 10 minutes.
2. In a separate large bowl, mix together the potato starch, cornstarch, ½ cup (120 ml) of the water and the cooking oil. If the batter feels too stiff, stir in more water, 1 tablespoon (15 ml) at a time, to achieve a consistency like sweetened condensed milk. Add the pork to the batter and toss well to coat it.
3. In a deep skillet or wok, heat peanut oil to 350°F (175°C). A few pieces at a time, slide the pork into the hot oil and deep-fry it for 2 to 3 minutes. Remember that you will be deep-frying the pork again a second time, so don't overcook it the first time. Using a mesh strainer, collect the pork and shake off the excess oil. Transfer the pork to a wire rack or a large paper towel–lined plate. Deep-fry the rest of pork and let it rest on the rack or lined plate for 5 minutes. Reserve the deep-frying oil.
4. For the sauce, in a small bowl, combine 1½ cups (360 ml) of the water and the sugar, soy sauce, vinegar and salt and whisk well to dissolve the sugar; set aside. In a second small bowl, combine the potato starch and the remaining 3 tablespoons (45 g) of water and mix well; set aside.
5. In a skillet over high heat, heat 1 tablespoon (15 ml) of the reserved deep-frying oil. Sauté the onion, bell pepper and mushrooms, if using, for 1 minute. Add the cucumber and toss for 10 seconds. Pour in the sauce mixture and let it come to a boil. Add about two-thirds of the starch water and let it thicken. Add more starch water if you desire a thicker sauce consistency. Lower the heat to a simmer to keep the sauce warm while preparing to deep-fry the pork again.
6. Heat the reserved deep-frying oil again and deep-fry the pork for the second time, 2 to 3 minutes, or until the pieces turn golden brown and crisp. Shake off the excess oil from the pork and place the pork pieces on a serving platter. Pour the sauce over the pork and serve immediately.

The Korean Home Kitchen | 29

# Chuncheon-Style Spicy Chicken Stir-Fry

**Prep time: 10 minutes | Cook time: 30 minutes | Serves 4**

- 8 oz (225 g) Korean rice cake sticks
- 1 lb (455 g) boneless, skinless chicken thighs, diced
- 2 tbsp (30 ml) cooking oil
- 1 medium onion, sliced
- ½ small cabbage (about 13 oz [360 g]), diced
- 1 medium sweet potato (preferably Korean), cut into thin wedges
- 7 to 9 fresh perilla or basil leaves, sliced
- ¼ cup (60 ml) cola or chicken stock
- 1 small Asian leek, or 2 green onions, sliced
- 1 tbsp (8 g) toasted sesame seeds
- SAUCE
- 3 tbsp (49 g) Korean chili paste
- 2 to 3 tbsp (12 to 18 g) Korean chili flakes
- 3 tbsp (45 ml) soy sauce
- 2 cloves garlic, minced
- 1 tbsp (13 g) sugar
- 2 tsp (4 g) curry powder
- 2 tbsp (30 ml) sweet rice wine (mirin)
- 2 tsp (10 ml) sesame oil
- ½ tsp freshly ground black pepper
- 2 tbsp (30 ml) Korean oligo syrup or corn syrup (optional)

1. Soak the rice cakes in warm water for 10 minutes. If the rice cakes are fresh, skip the soaking. After 10 minutes, drain and set aside.
2. Meanwhile prepare the sauce. In a small bowl, combine all the sauce ingredients and mix well.
3. Place the chicken in a bowl, add 3 tablespoons (45 ml) of the sauce and toss together. Set aside.
4. Coat a large, heavy, lidded skillet or wok with cooking oil and place it over medium-high heat. Add the chicken, onion, cabbage, rice cakes, sweet potato wedges and perilla leaves. Drizzle the rest of the sauce over the vegetables.
5. When you hear the loud sizzling sound, stir-fry the mixture to ensure all the ingredients are coated with the sauce, about 2 minutes. Drizzle the cola over the mixture, cover it and cook for 5 minutes over medium heat.
6. Remove the cover. Add the leek and toss together. Stir-fry until the rice cakes and vegetables are tender, 2 to 3 minutes. Sprinkle with the sesame seeds and serve hot.

# Andong-Style Braised Chicken with Noodles

**Prep time: 15 minutes | Cook time: 50 minutes | Serves 6**

- 4 oz (115 g) Korean sweet potato noodles
- 1 (3-lb [1.4-kg]) chicken, cut into pieces, skin removed if possible
- 5 to 6 dried chiles
- 1 medium onion, sliced
- 2 to 3 medium carrots, peeled and cut into ½" (1.3-cm)-thick slices
- 10.6 oz (300 g) Yukon Gold potatoes, peeled and cut into ½" (1.3-cm)-thick slices
- 1 to 2 fresh green chiles, sliced
- 1 green onion, finely chopped, for garnish
- 2 tsp (5 g) toasted sesame seeds, for garnish
- Cooked rice, for serving
- BROWN SUGAR SOY SAUCE
- ½ cup (120 ml) soy sauce
- 2 tbsp (30 ml) oyster sauce
- 1 cup (240 ml) water
- ¼ cup (56 g) dark brown sugar
- 3 cloves garlic, minced
- 1 tsp pureed fresh ginger
- 1 tsp freshly ground black pepper

1. Soak the sweet potato noodles in warm water for 20 minutes; set aside.
2. Bring a large pot of water to a boil over high heat. Add the chicken pieces and boil them for 3 minutes. Remove the chicken and discard the water. Place the chicken in a colander; set aside.
3. In a small bowl, mix together all the sauce ingredients. The cocoa powder won't mix in very well and that is okay.
4. Return the chicken to the empty pot and add the dried chiles. If you want to increase the spiciness, break a few of the dried chiles to release their seeds. Pour the sauce mixture over the chicken, cover it and cook for 10 minutes over medium heat, or until the chicken is mostly cooked.
5. Turn the chicken over, making sure to coat it evenly with the sauce. Add the onion and carrots to the pot; stir, re-cover it and cook for another 7 to 8 minutes over medium heat. Add the potatoes and cover it again, but leave an opening for the steam to escape this time. Cook until the vegetables are almost tender, 3 to 5 minutes.
6. Drain the water from the sweet potato noodles and add them to the pot along with the fresh green chile. Increase the heat to medium-high and continue to cook, uncovered, for another 3 to 5 minutes, tossing occasionally.
7. When the vegetables are tender and the noodles are soft yet chewy, remove it from the heat. Let the stew sit for 5 minutes, uncovered, to allow the chicken and the noodles to soak up the flavor. Transfer the chicken, vegetables and noodles to a large serving platter and drizzle with the gravy. Garnish with the green onion and sesame seeds. Serve hot with a little bit of rice.

## Korean Chicken Salad

**Prep time: 5 minutes | Cook time: 35 minutes | Serves 6 TO 8**

- 3 boneless, skinless chicken breast halves
- 8 oz (225 g) mung bean sprouts
- Salt
- 1 small onion, thinly julienned
- 1 small red bell pepper, seeded and thinly julienned
- 1 small yellow pepper, seeded and thinly julienned
- ½ English cucumber, thinly julienned
- ¼ small red cabbage, shredded
- 1 sweet apple, thinly sliced
- 2 fresh perilla leaves, thinly julienned, for garnish (optional)
- MUSTARD DRESSING
- 2 tsp (10 g) prepared Korean mustard
- 1 tbsp (15 ml) soy sauce
- ¾ tsp salt
- ¼ cup (60 ml) fresh lemon juice
- ¼ cup (84 g) honey
- 2 tsp (10 ml) sesame oil
- 1 clove garlic, finely minced
- 2 tbsp (16 g) toasted sesame seeds, crushed

1. Poach the chicken breast in simmering water over low heat, about 20 minutes, until tender. Let the chicken cool a little and shred it to bite size. Cover it and chill in the refrigerator.
2. Bring a pot of water to a boil and blanch the mung bean sprouts with some salt for 10 seconds. Using a colander, drain and rinse with cold water. Chill in the refrigerator.
3. Meanwhile, prepare the dressing. In a small bowl, combine all the dressing ingredients and whisk well. Chill in the refrigerator.
4. On a large serving platter, arrange the salad ingredients in a pleasing pattern, placing the shredded chicken in the center and garnishing with the perilla leaves, if using.
5. To serve, divide the salad among individual serving dishes and drizzle with the dressing. Toss and serve immediately.

## Spicy Seafood & Bean Sprouts

**Prep time: 5 minutes | Cook time: 15 minutes | Serves 6**

- 6 large dried anchovies, deveined, head removed
- 3 cups (720 ml) water
- 1 lb (455 g) soybean sprouts, cleaned
- 2 tbsp (30 ml) Korean soy sauce for soup
- 2 tbsp (30 ml) sweet rice wine (mirin)
- ¼ cup (25 g) Korean chili flakes
- 2 tbsp (33 g) Korean chili paste
- 2 tsp (9 g) sugar
- 1 tsp pureed fresh ginger
- 1 tbsp (10 g) finely minced garlic
- ½ tsp freshly ground black pepper
- 3 lb (1.4 kg) assorted seafood (crab, mussels, squid, shrimp), cleaned and cut
- ¼ cup (32 g) potato starch
- ¼ cup (60 ml) water
- 2 tsp (10 ml) sesame oil (optional)
- 1 tbsp (8 g) sesame seeds, for garnish
- 1 green onion, finely chopped, for garnish

1. In a large, lidded pan or wok, combine the dried anchovies and water and add the bean sprouts on top; do not mix. Cover it and bring to a boil. Lower the heat to low and let it simmer for 3 to 4 minutes. Using kitchen tongs, transfer the bean sprouts to a strainer; set aside. Pick out the anchovies and discard them; reserve the stock in the pan.
2. In a small bowl, combine the soy sauce, rice wine, chili flakes, chili paste, sugar, ginger, garlic, black pepper and ¼ cup (60 ml) of the reserved stock to create a chili sauce; mix well and set aside.
3. Bring the remaining stock to a boil again over medium-high heat. Add the crab pieces first, cover it and cook for 2 to 3 minutes. Add the rest of the seafood and cover it with the soybean sprouts. Drizzle the chili sauce over the top and cover it again. Cook over medium-high heat for 3 to 4 minutes.
4. In another small bowl, combine the potato starch with the water and mix well.
5. Lift the lid and, using tongs or a spatula, stir the seafood and soybean sprouts in the chili sauce until it's mixed thoroughly. Add about two-thirds of the starch mixture to the pan and continue to cook over medium-high heat to thicken. Add more of the starch mixture until the sauce is your desired consistency.
6. Remove the pan from the heat. Drizzle the sesame oil, if using, on the top and sprinkle with the sesame seeds and green onion. Serve immediately.

# Chapter 7
# Fish and Seafood

## Spicy Marinated Crabs

**Prep time: 15 minutes | Cook time: 2 hours | Serves 4**

3 tablespoons soy sauce
¼ cup (30 g) gochugaru
1 tablespoon minced garlic
1 teaspoon minced peeled fresh ginger
1 tablespoon packed dark brown sugar
2 teaspoons toasted sesame seeds
1 teaspoon fish sauce
½ cup (50 g) thinly sliced scallions or leeks, white parts only
1 small carrot, julienned
1 pound (455 g) cleaned blue crabs

1. Combine everything but the crabs in a small mixing bowl. Whisk until well combined and the sugar is dissolved.
2. Toss each crab with the sauce until it is coated, then place it in a large mixing bowl.
3. Once all the crabs are covered with the marinade, pour the remaining marinade over the crabs, and let the bowl sit out, covered, for 1 to 2 hours, then refrigerate it overnight.
4. Serve the crabs within 3 days.

## Pan-Fried Fish Fillets

**Prep time: 10 minutes | Cook time: 15 minutes | Serves 4**

- 1 pound fresh flounder or cod, rinsed, patted dry, and cut into 2-inch pieces
- 1 tablespoon sea salt, divided
- 2 eggs
- 1 teaspoon freshly ground black pepper
- 3 tablespoons flour
- 1 tablespoon vegetable oil
- Sensational Soy Dipping Sauce (optional)

1. Lightly salt the fish on all sides.
2. In a medium shallow bowl, whisk the eggs with the remaining salt and the pepper.
3. Put the flour in another shallow bowl next to the egg mixture.
4. Heat a bit of the vegetable oil in a medium skillet over medium heat. Dip each fish piece first into the flour to coat, then into the egg mixture, and then gently put it in the skillet. Don't crowd the pan. You might have to do this in batches, adding more oil as necessary.
5. Serve with soy dipping sauce, if desired.

## Spicy Marinated Squid

**Prep time:** 20 minutes, plus 2 hours to marinate | **Cook time:** 6 minutes | **Serves 4**

- 2 pounds squid, thawed if frozen, cleaned, body and tentacles separated
- 2 tablespoons gochujang
- 1 tablespoon coarse gochugaru flakes
- 1 tablespoon minced garlic
- 1 tablespoon plum syrup
- 1 tablespoon toasted sesame oil
- 1 tablespoon rice vinegar
- 2 teaspoons kosher salt

1. Pat the squid dry with a paper towel.
2. In a large bowl, whisk together the gochujang, gochugaru, garlic, plum syrup, oil, vinegar, and salt. Add the squid and combine until the marinade is evenly incorporated. Cover and refrigerate the bowl and let the squid marinate for 2 hours.
3. When you're ready to grill, shake off and discard any excess marinade from the squid.
4. Grill the squid over medium-high heat for about 3 minutes per side. The middle of the squid should be opaque. Use scissors to cut the squid into bite-size pieces.

## Rice & Fish Lettuce Wraps
**Prep time: 5 minutes | Cook time: 15 minutes | Serves 4**

- 2 tsp (10 ml) cooking oil
- ½ small onion, finely chopped
- 1 tbsp (10 g) minced garlic
- ½ (2-oz [56-g]) zucchini, finely chopped
- ½ cup (120 ml) water
- 2 tbsp (33 g) Korean fermented soybean paste
- 1 tbsp (16 g) Korean chili paste
- 1 tbsp (15 ml) soy sauce
- ½ tsp sugar
- 1 (14-oz [400-g]) can mackerel pike, drained, 3 tbsp (45 ml) liquid reserved
- 1 to 2 green chiles, sliced
- 1 green onion, chopped
- Freshly ground black pepper
- Assorted lettuce, such as Bibb, romaine, or green leaf, for serving
- Cooked rice, for serving
- Steamed cabbage and/or pumpkin leaves, for serving
- Perilla leaves, for serving

1. In a small pot, heat the oil over medium-high heat. Add the onion and garlic and cook until soft, 2 to 3 minutes. Add the zucchini and cook for another minute.
2. Add the water and, using a wooden spoon, smear the soybean and chili pastes into the pot until they're mixed into the water. Add the soy sauce, sugar, canned fish and its reserved liquid to the pot, breaking the fish into large chunks with the spoon. Add the green chile and bring the sauce to a boil, then simmer it for 7 to 8 minutes over medium-low heat, or until the sauce thickens. Remove it from the heat, and add the green onion, black pepper and stir; the sauce will thicken further as it cools.
3. Arrange the assorted lettuce leaves on a large serving platter or in a basket. Put the fish mixture in a small bowl.
4. To serve, put a spoonful of rice on a lettuce, cabbage, pumpkin or perilla leaf, or a combination of 2 to 3 leaves, and top with a tablespoon (15 ml) of the sauce. Close the lettuce to cover the rice and topping and put it into your mouth. Savor this little piece of heaven!

## Marinated Shrimp

**Prep time: 15 minutes, plus 2 hours to marinate | Cook time: 4 minutes | Serves 4**

- 1 pound large raw shrimp
- ¼ cup soy sauce
- 2 tablespoons lightly packed dark brown sugar
- 1 tablespoon coarse gochugaru flakes
- 2 tablespoons minced garlic

1. Peel the shrimp, if desired. Devein the shrimp by lightly cutting the top of the shrimp from head to tail and removing the dark line. Rinse under cold water, and pat dry with paper towels.
2. In a large bowl, whisk together the soy sauce, brown sugar, gochugaru, and garlic. Add the shrimp and combine until the marinade is evenly incorporated. Cover and refrigerate the bowl and let the shrimp marinate for no more than 2 hours.
3. When you're ready to grill, shake off and discard any excess marinade from the shrimp. Grill the shrimp over medium-high heat for about 2 minutes per side. The middle of the shrimp should be opaque.

### Crab Cakes in Korea
**Prep time: 5 minutes | Cook time: 35 minutes | Serves 4**

- 1/4 cup mayonnaise
- 2 tbsps. chopped fresh cilantro
- 1 tbsp. chopped fresh ginger
- 2 tsps. Asian fish sauce (nuoc mam or nam pla)
- 1 (6 ounce) can crabmeat - drained, flaked and cartilage removed
- three ounces chopped shrimp
- 1 ½ cups fresh breadcrumbs, made from crustless French bread
- salt and pepper to taste
- 1 ½ tbsps. peanut oil

1. Combine crab, shrimp, bread crumbs, fresh ginger, mayonnaise, fish sauce and cilantro together in a bowl before adding salt and pepper.
2. Take 1 fourth of a cup of this mixture and place in a bowl containing the remaining bread crumbs, and make a patty out of it.
3. Do the same for the rest of the crab mixture.
4. Now fry your patties in in hot oil over medium heat for about 5 minutes each side.
5. Serve

## Spicy Shrimp Skewers
**Prep time: 15 minutes | Cook time: 45 minutes | Serves 4**

- 1 pound 16 to 20 count shrimp, about 20 pieces, peeled and deveined
- 3 tablespoons Korean chili paste
- ¼ cup sugar
- Juice of ½ lemon (about 1 tablespoon)
- 2 garlic cloves, minced
- 1 teaspoon peeled, minced ginger
- 1 scallion, trimmed and thinly sliced (white and light green parts)
- 1 tablespoon white sesame seeds
- 1 red bell pepper, seeded, cut into large chunks
- 1 large sweet onion, cut into large chunks

1. Combine all ingredients except bell pepper and onion in a 1-gallon zip-top plastic bag and allow the shrimp to marinate for about 30 minutes in the refrigerator. Reserve the marinade.
2. Using four wooden or metal skewers (soak them for 30 minutes pre-grilling if using wood), prepare kebabs of shrimp, green pepper, and sweet onion, alternating, until you have four to five shrimp per skewer.
3. Prepare a grill for direct cooking over high heat. Grill the skewers over direct heat for 2 minutes. Brush excess marinade over shrimp, and grill on the other side for 2 more minutes. Serve hot.

# Chapter 8
# Soups, Stews & Braises

## Ground Soybean Stew

**Prep time: 15 minutes | Cook time: 55 minutes | Serves 4**

- ½ cup dried soybeans
- 8 dried anchovies, guts and heads removed
- 1 (5-by-5-inch) piece dried kelp
- ¼ cup pine nuts (or any type of nut, up to a maximum of 1 cup)
- ⅓ cup chopped yellow onion
- 3 garlic cloves, minced
- 2 teaspoons sesame oil
- 6 ounces boneless pork shoulder, cut into bite-size pieces
- 1 cup kimchi (that has been ripened for at least 1 month), chopped
- 1 tablespoon soy sauce
- ½ teaspoon black pepper
- 2 tablespoons saeujeot (salted fermented shrimp) or fish sauce, or 2 teaspoons coarse sea salt
- 1 scallion, both white and green parts, chopped

1. Put the dried soybeans in a large bowl, and cover with 4 cups of water. Soak for at least 10 hours; the soybeans will expand and double in size.
2. When ready to cook, to make the anchovy broth, in the Instant Pot, combine the dried anchovies, kelp, and 4 cups of water. Lock the lid, and close the steam valve. Set the timer for 1 minute on High Pressure.
3. When the timer sounds, natural release the steam for 5 minutes. Open the lid. Reserving the liquid, strain the anchovies and kelp over a large bowl. Discard the solids.
4. Drain and rinse the soaked soybeans. You will need to repeat this process a couple of times so that the skins come off the beans. It's okay to eat the skins, and there is no need to discard all the skins.
5. Put the beans, 1 cup of water, and the pine nuts in a high-speed blender. Puree until smooth. You will have about 2 cups of creamy soybeans.
6. Press the Sauté button, and set to High.
7. Once the screen reads HOT, in the Instant Pot, combine the onion, garlic, and oil. Cook for 1 minute.
8. Add the pork, kimchi, soy sauce, and pepper. Cook, stirring occasionally, for about 10 minutes, or until the pork has browned and the kimchi has turned a little soft. Turn off the Sauté mode.
9. Add the soybean mix and saeujeot, then pour in the anchovy broth. If it's too thick, add ⅓ cup of water (it should be the consistency of porridge). Lock the lid, and close the steam valve. Set the timer for 3 minutes on High Pressure.
10. When the timer sounds, natural release the steam for 6 minutes. Open the lid.
11. Add the scallions, and lightly stir. Ladle the stew into a bowl. Serve immediately.

## Braised Kimchi and Pork Belly
**Prep time: 15 minutes | Cook time: 40 minutes | Serves 4**

- 4 cups kimchi, cut into bite-size pieces
- 1 cup kimchi pickling liquid (optional)
- 1½ pounds pork belly, cut into bite-size pieces
- 3 tablespoons gochugaru (Korean red chili flakes)
- 2 tablespoons minced garlic
- 1½ tablespoons soy sauce
- 1 tablespoon grated fresh ginger
- 1 tablespoon doenjang (fermented soybean paste)
- 1 teaspoon granulated white sugar
- 1½ cups vegetable broth, or rice water (obtained from rinsing rice)
- 2 scallions, both white and green parts, chopped

1. Press the Sauté button, and set to High.
2. Once the screen reads HOT, put the kimchi in the Instant Pot. Cook for 5 minutes.
3. Add the kimchi pickling liquid (if using). Turn off the Sauté mode.
4. Add the pork belly, gochugaru, garlic, soy sauce, ginger, doenjang, and sugar, followed by the broth. Lock the lid, and close the steam valve. Set the timer for 10 minutes on High Pressure.
5. When the timer sounds, natural release the steam for 10 minutes. Open the lid.
6. Stir in the scallions. Ladle the pork and kimchi into a large bowl. Serve family-style with rice.

## Rice Cake Soup

**Prep time:** 10 minutes, plus 20 minutes to soak | **Cook time:** 55 minutes | **Serves 4**

- FOR THE BEEF BROTH
- 8 ounces beef stew meat
- 5 garlic cloves, peeled
- ½ yellow onion
- FOR THE BROTH CONTENTS
- 4 garlic cloves, minced
- 3 scallions, both white and green parts, chopped, divided
- 3 tablespoons soup soy sauce
- 2 tablespoons sesame oil
- 1 tablespoon sesame seeds
- 1 tablespoon coarse sea salt
- 1 teaspoon black pepper
- 1 pound tteokguk tteok soaked in water for 20 minutes and drained
- 2 large eggs, beaten
- 1 sheet roasted Korean seaweed (gim), crumbled

1. To Make the Broth: In the Instant Pot, combine the beef, 6 cups of water, the garlic, and onion. Lock the lid, and close the steam valve. Set the timer for 15 minutes on High Pressure.
   When the timer sounds, natural release the steam for 10 minutes, then quick release the remainder. Open the lid.
2. Remove the beef, garlic, and onion. The broth should remain in the Instant Pot. Reserve the beef, let cool, and discard the onion and garlic.
3. Press the Sauté button, and set to High. Bring the broth to a boil.
   To Make the Broth Contents: Cut the cooled beef into 1½-inch strips.
4. In a bowl, combine the beef, garlic, 2 scallions, the soup soy sauce, oil, sesame seeds, salt, and pepper. Mix well.
5. Once the broth is boiling, add the tteokguk tteok, and cook for about 5 minutes, or until soft.
6. Add the eggs, and turn off the Instant Pot. Ladle the tteokguk tteok and broth into a bowl.
7. Top with the seasoned beef, seaweed, and remaining scallion.

## Oxtail Soup

**Prep time: 10 minutes, plus 6 hours to soak and chill | Cook time: 1 hour 15 minutes | Serves 4**

- 3 pounds sliced oxtail
- 1 pound Korean radish or daikon, halved lengthwise and into ½-inch-thick semicircles
- 6 garlic cloves, peeled
- 5 scallions, both white and green parts, chopped
- Coarse sea salt
- Black pepper
- Cooked rice, for serving

1. In a large bowl, rinse the oxtail in cold running water; discard any bone fragments. Cover with water, and refrigerate for at least 6 hours. Change the water every 2 hours. Drain the oxtail, and transfer to the Instant Pot.
2. Add 4 cups of water. Lock the lid, and close the steam valve. Set the timer for 3 minutes on High Pressure.
3. When the timer sounds, natural release the steam for 6 minutes. Open the lid. Discard all the water, and rinse the oxtail under cold running water. Wash the pot clean so there is no scum or fat.
4. Return the oxtail to the Instant Pot, and add the radish, garlic, and 8 cups of water. Lock the lid, and close the steam valve. Set the timer for 25 minutes on High Pressure.
5. When the timer sounds, natural release the steam for 10 minutes. Open the lid. Ladle the soup and oxtail into bowls.
6. Top with the scallions. Add salt and pepper to taste. Serve the dish with rice.

## Kimchi Stew

**Prep time: 5 minutes | Cook time: 55 minutes | Serves 4**

- 1 tablespoon canola, vegetable, or corn oil
- 2½ cups kimchi, chopped into bite-size pieces
- 8 ounces pork ribs or 1 (12-ounce) can luncheon meat like Spam, cut into 1-inch-thick slices
- 3 tablespoons gochugaru (Korean red chili flakes)
- 4 teaspoons minced garlic
- ½ cup kimchi pickling liquid (optional)
- 2 teaspoons fish sauce
- 2 teaspoons soy sauce
- 1 teaspoon granulated white sugar
- 1 (14-ounce) package medium firm tofu, cut into ½-inch-thick slices
- 3 scallions, both white and green parts, chopped
- Cooked rice, for serving

1. Press the Sauté button, and set to High.
2. Once the screen reads HOT, in the Instant Pot, combine the oil and kimchi. Sauté for 3 minutes.
3. Add the pork, 4 cups of water, the gochugaru, garlic, kimchi pickling liquid (if using), fish sauce, soy sauce, and sugar. Cook for 10 minutes. Turn off the Sauté mode. Lock the lid, and close the steam valve. Set the timer for 10 minutes on High Pressure.
4. When the timer sounds, natural release the steam for 15 minutes.
5. Open the lid. Press the Sauté button, and set to High. Bring the stew to a boil, about 5 minutes.
6. Add the tofu, and cook for 2 minutes.
7. Add the scallions, and turn off the Instant Pot. Serve the stew immediately with rice.

## Seaweed Soup

**Prep time: 5 minutes, plus 20 minutes to soak | Cook time: 50 minutes | Serves 4**

- 1½ grams (0.05 ounces) dried wakame or dried sea mustard
- 1 tablespoon sesame oil, plus 1 teaspoon
- 8 ounces beef brisket, round, or skirt steak, cut into bite-size pieces
- 1 teaspoon minced garlic
- 2 tablespoons soup soy sauce
- ½ teaspoon fish sauce

1. Put the dried seaweed in a large bowl, and cover in room-temperature water. Soak for 20 minutes. Then drain and rinse several times in cold running water. Drain once more, and squeeze the water out. Cut into bite-size pieces.
2. Press the Sauté button, and set to High.
3. Once the screen reads HOT, in the Instant Pot, combine 1 tablespoon of oil, the beef, and garlic. Cook for 5 minutes, or until the beef has browned.
4. Add the seaweed. Sauté for 2 minutes.
5. Add 6 cups of water, the soup soy sauce, and fish sauce. Turn off the Sauté mode. Lock the lid, and close the steam valve. Set the timer for 20 minutes on High Pressure.
6. When the timer sounds, natural release the steam for 10 minutes. Open the lid. Ladle the soup into a bowl.
7. Drizzle with the remaining 1 teaspoon of oil before serving.

# Chapter 9
# Barbecue: Grilled, Smoked & Fired

## Octopus

**Prep time: 5 minutes | Cook time: about 3 hours | Serves 4 to 6**

- FOR THE OCTOPUS
- 1 small (12- to 16-ounce/340 to 455 g) whole octopus
- 2 tablespoons canola oil
- Kosher salt
- FOR SERVING
- Lettuces and Herbs
- Kimchi Vinaigrette
- Scallion Salad
- Ssam Jang
- 2 to 3 Banchan
- Rice

1. Preheat the oven to 250°F (120°C).
2. Bring a large saucepan of water to a boil over high heat. Add the octopus and let it cook for 1 minute, then remove it to a baking pan.
3. Place the octopus in the oven and let it cook until it is tender when you pierce it with the tip of a knife, about 2 to 3 hours.
4. Slice off the head and discard it, then separate each tentacle where it begins at the neck.
5. In a large skillet or grill pan, heat 1 tablespoon of the oil over medium heat.
6. Season the octopus tentacles liberally with salt on both sides. Toss with the remaining tablespoon of oil to coat.
7. When the skillet is hot, add the octopus. Cook until it is charred on both sides, about 3 minutes per side.
8. Cut the octopus tentacles into bite-size pieces, and serve immediately with the lettuces and herbs, kimchi vinaigrette or ssam jang, scallion salad, banchan, and rice.

## Shrimp and Squid

**Prep time: 5 minutes | Cook time: 15 minutes | Serves 4 to 6**

- FOR THE SHRIMP
- 2 tablespoons canola oil
- 1 pound (450 g) fresh medium-size shrimp, peeled and deveined OR 1 pound (455 g) fresh, unfrozen squid bodies and tentacles, cleaned
- Kosher salt
- FOR SERVING
- Lettuces and Herbs
- Scallion Salad
- Kimchi Vinaigrette
- Ssam Jang
- 2 to 3 Banchan
- Rice

1. In a large skillet or grill pan, heat 1 tablespoon of the oil over medium heat.
2. Season the shrimp or squid lightly with salt on both sides. Toss with the remaining tablespoon of oil to coat.
3. When the skillet is hot, add the shrimp or squid. Cook until they just begin to curl, about a minute per side, then remove them to a serving platter. Cut the squid, if using, into bite-size pieces.
4. Serve immediately with the lettuces and herbs, scallion salad, kimchi vinaigrette or ssam jang, banchan, and rice.

## BBQ Pork Belly

**Prep time: 5 minutes | Cook time: 1 hour 45 minutes | Serves 4**

- ½ large yellow onion, sliced
- 2 garlic cloves, sliced
- 1 teaspoon vegetable oil
- 1 pound skin-on pork belly, cut into 2-inch cubes
- 4 dried shiitake mushrooms, sliced
- 1 cup water or chicken stock
- 2 tablespoons light brown sugar
- 2 tablespoons soy sauce
- 1 teaspoon fish sauce
- 1 tablespoon rice wine vinegar
- 3 cups Napa cabbage (about 5 to 6 leaves), halved lengthwise, then rough-chopped
- 3 Korean chili peppers, seeded and chopped into large rings

1. In a large pot, sweat the onion and garlic in vegetable oil over medium heat.
2. Add the pork belly, plus all remaining ingredients aside from the Napa cabbage and Korean chili peppers, reduce the heat to medium low, cover, and cook for 1½ hours, until the pork belly is tender and a good amount of its fat has been rendered.
3. Add the cabbage and chili peppers and cook for 5 additional minutes, with the lid on, to steam them. Stir everything together before serving.

## Braised Pork Belly

**Prep time: 5 minutes | Cook time: about 2 hours | Serves 4**

- 2 pounds skin-on pork belly, cut into long, 2- to 3-inch thick strips
- 3 cups water
- Two 12-ounce pilsner beers (I use Budweiser)
- 5 dried shiitake mushrooms
- 3 garlic cloves, smashed
- 2 scallions, trimmed and cut into 2-inch pieces (white and light green parts)
- 1 tablespoon fish sauce
- 2 tablespoons soy sauce
- 1 tablespoon fermented bean paste
- ¼ cup mirin
- 1 cinnamon stick
- ¼ teaspoon ground white pepper

1. Add the pork belly to a large pot, cover with water, and boil for 5 minutes. Remove the pork belly and rinse under cold water, discard the water, and scrub out the pot—this will help remove any funky "barnyard" odors and flavors.
2. Add the pork, the 3 cups fresh water, and all other ingredients to the pot, bring to a boil, then reduce the heat to medium-low and simmer, covered, for 1½ hours (or longer, if you prefer).
3. Slice the pork belly thin and serve it with Korean Chili Sauce and steamed Napa cabbage.

### Beef and Tofu Meatballs

**Prep time: 5 minutes | Cook time: 15 minutes | Serves 4 (makes roughly 20 to 24 meatballs)**

- 1 pound ground beef
- ¼ pack (roughly 4 ounces) firm tofu, drained and crumbled
- ½ medium yellow onion, minced
- 1 medium carrot, peeled and minced (about ¼ cup)
- 2 scallions, trimmed and sliced (white and light green parts)
- 2 garlic cloves, minced
- 1 tablespoon sesame oil
- 1 teaspoon kosher salt
- ½ teaspoon freshly ground black pepper
- ½ cup all-purpose flour
- 3 eggs, vigorously beaten
- 2 tablespoons vegetable oil, plus more if necessary, for panfrying

1. In a large bowl, combine all ingredients except flour, eggs, and vegetable oil and mix well. Make sure the tofu is crumbled into fine pieces so it fully incorporates into the ground beef; this helps bind the "balls" together. Form portions of the beef mixture into small, round patties about the size of a golf ball, collect them on a sheet tray or plate, then smash each down lightly with your palm or a spatula.
2. Place the flour and beaten eggs into two separate bowls. Add the vegetable oil to a sauté pan over medium heat. Working in modest batches to avoid overcrowding, dredge a handful of meatballs in flour, shake off any excess, then quickly dip each in the beaten eggs before adding them to the hot pan.
3. Fry each batch of meatballs until cooked though, about 4 minutes per side, transferring them to cool and dry on paper towels. Repeat with the remaining meatballs, adding additional vegetable oil to the pan if necessary.

## Marinated Skirt Steak
**Prep time: 5 minutes | Cook time: 15 minutes | Serves 4**

- 1 pound skirt steak, cut into 4 even pieces
- 1 medium yellow onion, sliced
- 4 garlic cloves, sliced
- 4 scallions, trimmed and cut into 1-inch pieces (white and light green parts)
- 8 dried shiitake mushrooms
- 2 tablespoons soy sauce
- 2 tablespoons sesame oil
- 2 teaspoons kosher salt
- 4 tablespoons maple syrup
- 4 tablespoons water

1. Combine all the ingredients in a bowl and mix together well, coating the meat. Transfer everything to a 1-gallon zip-top plastic bag and marinate, refrigerated, for a minimum of 12 hours, ideally overnight. The next day, drain the marinade.
2. Heat an oiled grill pan over medium-high heat, then add the vegetables and steak. Cook the steaks for 2 minutes per side, and allow them to rest for 4 to 5 minutes before slicing them against the grain.
3. Remove the vegetables once they are nicely caramelized. You can also prepare this dish on an outdoor grill using indirect heat. Eat with lettuce wraps, steamed rice, Korean Chili Sauce, and your pick of banchan.

## BBQ Beef Short Ribs

**Prep time: 5 minutes | Cook time: 15 minutes | Serves 4**

- 2 pounds Korean-style beef short ribs, cross-cut, 1 inch thick
- ½ cup soy sauce
- ¼ cup light brown sugar, packed
- 1 large Asian pear, peeled and chopped
- 3 garlic cloves
- 1 tablespoon mirin
- 1 tablespoon sesame oil
- 1 tablespoon peeled, chopped ginger
- ½ medium yellow onion, chopped
- 1 tablespoon vegetable oil, plus more for grilling

1. Rinse the short ribs with cold water and be sure to remove any bone shards. Place all ingredients aside from the beef in a blender and puree until smooth.
2. Combine the beef and the puree in a 1-gallon zip-top plastic bag or large sealable container and marinate for 24 to 48 hours.
3. Remove the short ribs from the marinade (discard the marinade) and pat off any excess liquid with a paper towel. Rub the ribs lightly with additional vegetable oil and grill them over indirect heat for 10 minutes. The beef should be well done, as the marinade will keep it moist and tender. Serve with steamed rice and banchan.

## Roasted Cauliflower

**Prep time: 5 minutes | Cook time: 1 hour 15 minutes | Serves 4**

- 3 tablespoons Korean chili paste
- 2 tablespoons fermented bean paste
- 2 tablespoons rice wine vinegar
- 2 tablespoons mirin
- 2 tablespoons raw sugar
- 1 tablespoon soy sauce
- 1 tablespoon sesame oil
- 1 head cauliflower, trimmed of leaves, bottom sliced flat, and halved lengthwise

1. Whisk all ingredients except the cauliflower in a mixing bowl to make a marinade. Transfer to a 1-gallon zip-top plastic bag, add the cauliflower halves, and refrigerate for 24 hours.
2. Preheat the oven to 375°F. Add ½ cup of water to the bottom of an oven-safe roasting pan, then transfer the marinated cauliflower to the center of the pan, reserving any excess marinade.
3. Roast the cauliflower for 30 minutes, then remove it from the oven and use a brush or spoon to baste it with the reserved marinade.
4. Add another ½ cup of water to the bottom of the pan, turn the cauliflower then roast it for an additional 30 minutes. Allow the cauliflower to rest for 15 minutes before slicing it and serving it warm with lettuce wraps and steamed rice.

### BBQ King Oyster Mushrooms
**Prep time: 5 minutes | Cook time: 25 minutes | Serves 4**

- 3 tablespoons soy sauce
- 1 tablespoons sesame oil
- 2 tablespoons maple syrup
- 1 tablespoon Dijon mustard
- 2 garlic cloves, sliced
- 1 tablespoon mirin
- 1 tablespoon rice wine vinegar
- 1 tablespoon fermented bean paste
- 1 tablespoon water
- 1 pound king oyster mushrooms, cut in half lengthwise

1. Whisk all ingredients except the mushrooms in a bowl. Collect the mushrooms in a 1-gallon zip-top plastic bag, pour in the contents of the bowl, and marinate at room temperature for 4 hours, or in the refrigerator for 12 to 24 hours.
2. Reserve the marinade for basting. Grill over direct heat for 2 minutes per side, then shift to indirect heat for 20 minutes with the grill lid closed, basting the mushrooms with the leftover marinade during grilling.
3. If you don't want to cook over gas or charcoal, use a grill pan, sauté pan, or roast in the oven at 400°F to get color. Serve hot, cold, or room temperature, with steamed rice, as banchan, or cut up as an addition to a soup or stew.

# Chapter 10
# Sweets, Desserts and Drinks

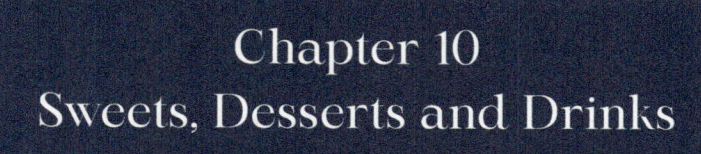

## Sweet Pancakes With Cinnamon Brown Sugar Filling

**Prep time:** 5 minutes | **Cook time:** 15 minutes | **Makes about 8 to 10 hotteok**

- DOUGH
- 2½ cups (313 g) all-purpose flour
- ½ cup (79 g) sweet rice flour
- 1 tsp sugar
- 1 tsp salt
- 2 tsp (8 g) instant yeast
- ½ tsp baking powder
- 1¼ cups (300 ml) whole milk, lukewarm
- 3 tbsp (42 g) unsalted butter, melted
- Oil, for hands and frying
- CINNAMON BROWN SUGAR FILLING
- ⅔ cup (150 g) light brown sugar
- 1 tsp ground cinnamon
- ½ tbsp (4 g) all-purpose flour
- ¼ cup (35 g) finely chopped roasted peanuts

1. In a large bowl, stir together the flours, sugar, salt, yeast and baking powder. Pour in the milk and the melted butter; mix well with a wooden spoon. Continue to stir the dough with the wooden spoon for 2 minutes to develop the gluten.
2. Cover the dough with a damp towel and let it sit in a warm place for 1 to 2 hours, or until it's doubled in volume.
3. Meanwhile, prepare the filling. In a bowl, mix together the brown sugar, cinnamon, flour and peanuts. Set aside.
4. When the dough has doubled in volume, punch down the dough and let it rest for a few more minutes. Keep a small bowl with a little bit of oil on the side to oil your hands.
5. On a griddle, heat 2 tablespoons (30 ml) of oil over medium-low heat. Oil your hands, take a piece of the dough (about one-eighth to one-tenth of the total amount) and flatten it in your palm. Using a round spoon, place a heaping tablespoon (18 g) of the filling in the center of the dough. Gather the dough around the filling and pinch it to seal the filling inside.
6. Place the dough seam side down on the hot griddle and let it sear for 30 seconds. Flip the dough to the other side and press down with a greased hotteok press or spatula to flatten it to about a ½-inch (1.3-cm) thickness. Do not press down too much; if it gets too thin, the dough will tear easily. Panfry for 1 to 2 minutes, or until it's golden brown. Then, flip to the other side again and continue to cook until it's golden brown and crisp. Drizzle more oil on the griddle, as needed, and adjust the heat level so that you don't brown the crust too quickly. Repeat to cook the remaining dough.
7. Serve hot and be careful not to burn your tongue.

## Watermelon Punch

**Prep time:** 15 minutes | **Cook time:** 5 minutes | **Serves 8**

- 9 cups cubed watermelon (from about 2 large watermelons)
- 2 cups balled watermelon (from about ½ small watermelon)
- 1 cup balled cantaloupe (from about ½ large cantaloupe)
- 1 cup quartered strawberries
- 4 cups ginger ale
- Ice cubes, for chilling and serving

1. In a blender, blend the watermelon cubes to make about 2 cups of watermelon juice.
2. In a punch bowl or pitcher combine the watermelon balls, cantaloupe balls, and strawberries. Add the ginger ale, then the watermelon juice. Fill the bowl or pitcher with ice cubes and serve immediately.

## Korean Cinnamon Punch

**Prep time:** 10 minutes, plus 9 hours to chill | **Cook time:** 1 hour | **Serves 4**

- 5 cinnamon sticks
- ½ cup peeled and coarsely sliced fresh ginger
- 8 cups water
- 1 cup lightly packed dark brown sugar
- 2 dried whole persimmons, quartered
- 12 or 20 pine nuts, for serving
- Ice, for serving

1. In a medium pot over high heat, combine the cinnamon, ginger, and water and bring to a boil. Cover the pot, reduce the heat to medium-low, and simmer for 45 minutes.
2. Add the sugar and continue to simmer for 15 minutes more, stirring to make sure the sugar dissolves.
3. Remove the pot from the heat. Discard the cinnamon sticks and ginger and add the dried persimmons.
4. Let the punch cool to room temperature for about 1 hour. Then, pour it into a pitcher with a lid and chill it in the refrigerator for 9 hours or overnight.
5. When you're ready to serve, place 3 to 5 pine nuts and the ice in each of four glasses before pouring the punch.

## Cinnamon-Sugar Rice Cakes

**Prep time: 5 minutes | Cook time: 15 minutes | Serves 4**

- ½ of the Crispy Rice Cakes recipe, before boiling and pan-searing
- 1½ cups sugar
- 1 tablespoon plus 1 teaspoon ground cinnamon
- 2 teaspoons ground ginger
- ½ teaspoon kosher salt

1. Cut the rice cakes into small balls, about the size of a donut hole. Combine the remaining ingredients in a bowl and set aside.
2. Bring a medium pot of water to a boil, reduce to a steady simmer, then poach the rice cakes for about 10 minutes.
3. Remove the cakes with a slotted spoon and drain well before gently transferring them to the cinnamon-sugar bowl.
4. Toss the poached rice cakes with the mixture to coat them evenly, and allow them to cool slightly before serving.

## No-Churn Korean Instant Coffee Ice Cream

**Prep time: 10 minutes, plus 6 hours to freeze | Cook time: 5 minutes | Makes 6 cups**

- 1 (14-ounce) can sweetened condensed milk
- 2 tablespoons Korean instant coffee
- 1 teaspoon kosher salt
- 2 cups heavy (whipping) cream

1. In a medium bowl, mix together the condensed milk, Korean instant coffee, and salt.
2. In a separate larger bowl, use a hand mixer to whisk the cream for 3 to 5 minutes, until stiff peaks form.
3. Gently fold the condensed milk mixture into the whipped cream.
4. Pour the mixture into a 9-by-5-inch loaf pan, cover it with plastic wrap, and place it in the refrigerator for 6 hours, or until hardened.
5. Scoop out the ice cream when you're ready to serve.

# Appendix 1 Measurement Conversion Chart

| Volume Equivalents (Dry) ||
|---|---|
| **US STANDARD** | **METRIC (APPROXIMATE)** |
| 1/8 teaspoon | 0.5 mL |
| 1/4 teaspoon | 1 mL |
| 1/2 teaspoon | 2 mL |
| 3/4 teaspoon | 4 mL |
| 1 teaspoon | 5 mL |
| 1 tablespoon | 15 mL |
| 1/4 cup | 59 mL |
| 1/2 cup | 118 mL |
| 3/4 cup | 177 mL |
| 1 cup | 235 mL |
| 2 cups | 475 mL |
| 3 cups | 700 mL |
| 4 cups | 1 L |

| Weight Equivalents ||
|---|---|
| **US STANDARD** | **METRIC (APPROXIMATE)** |
| 1 ounce | 28 g |
| 2 ounces | 57 g |
| 5 ounces | 142 g |
| 10 ounces | 284 g |
| 15 ounces | 425 g |
| 16 ounces (1 pound) | 455 g |
| 1.5 pounds | 680 g |
| 2 pounds | 907 g |

| Volume Equivalents (Liquid) |||
|---|---|---|
| **US STANDARD** | **US STANDARD (OUNCES)** | **METRIC (APPROXIMATE)** |
| 2 tablespoons | 1 fl.oz. | 30 mL |
| 1/4 cup | 2 fl.oz. | 60 mL |
| 1/2 cup | 4 fl.oz. | 120 mL |
| 1 cup | 8 fl.oz. | 240 mL |
| 1 1/2 cup | 12 fl.oz. | 355 mL |
| 2 cups or 1 pint | 16 fl.oz. | 475 mL |
| 4 cups or 1 quart | 32 fl.oz. | 1 L |
| 1 gallon | 128 fl.oz. | 4 L |

| Temperatures Equivalents ||
|---|---|
| **FAHRENHEIT(F)** | **CELSIUS(C) APPROXIMATE)** |
| 225 °F | 107 °C |
| 250 °F | 120 ° °C |
| 275 °F | 135 °C |
| 300 °F | 150 °C |
| 325 °F | 160 °C |
| 350 °F | 180 °C |
| 375 °F | 190 °C |
| 400 °F | 205 °C |
| 425 °F | 220 °C |
| 450 °F | 235 °C |
| 475 °F | 245 °C |
| 500 °F | 260 °C |

# Appendix 2 The Dirty Dozen and Clean Fifteen

The Environmental Working Group (EWG) is a nonprofit, nonpartisan organization dedicated to protecting human health and the environment Its mission is to empower people to live healthier lives in a healthier environment. This organization publishes an annual list of the twelve kinds of produce, in sequence, that have the highest amount of pesticide residue-the Dirty Dozen-as well as a list of the fifteen kinds of produce that have the least amount of pesticide residue-the Clean Fifteen.

| THE DIRTY DOZEN ||
|---|---|
| The 2016 Dirty Dozen includes the following produce. These are considered among the year's most important produce to buy organic: ||
| Strawberries | Spinach |
| Apples | Tomatoes |
| Nectarines | Bell peppers |
| Peaches | Cherry tomatoes |
| Celery | Cucumbers |
| Grapes | Kale/collard greens |
| Cherries | Hot peppers |
| The Dirty Dozen list contains two additional items kale/collard greens and hot peppers-because they tend to contain trace levels of highly hazardous pesticides. ||

| THE CLEAN FIFTEEN ||
|---|---|
| The least critical to buy organically are the Clean Fifteen list. The following are on the 2016 list: ||
| Avocados | Papayas |
| Corn | Kiw |
| Pineapples | Eggplant |
| Cabbage | Honeydew |
| Sweet peas | Grapefruit |
| Onions | Cantaloupe |
| Asparagus | Cauliflower |
| Mangos | |
| Some of the sweet corn sold in the United States are made from genetically engineered (GE) seedstock. Buy organic varieties of these crops to avoid GE produce. ||

# Appendix 3 Index

## A
agave syrup .................................................. 46, 49
all-purpose flour ................................................ 46
almond ................................................... 50, 52, 53
almond flour ................................................ 22, 59
almond milk ....................................................... 53
apple ................................................................... 46
apple cider vinegar ............................. 21, 23, 58, 61
asparagus ........................................................... 26
avocado ................................. 21, 22, 24, 25, 27, 28, 58
]avocado oil ............................ 21, 22, 24, 25, 27, 58, 60

## B
baking powder ............................................ 46, 48
basmati rice ....................................................... 47
bread ...................................................... 49, 50, 51, 55
bread crumbs ..................................................... 48
Brioche bread .................................................... 50
broccoli ........................................................ 48, 60
brown rice .......................................................... 54
brown sugar .......................................... 46, 50, 55
Brussels sprout .................................................. 59
butter ................................ 27, 48, 51, 52, 54, 60

## C
carrot ................................................................. 53
cauliflower ............................... 27, 57, 58, 60, 61
cayenne pepper ................................................. 47
challah bread ..................................................... 51
Cheddar cheese ........................................... 54, 57
chia seeds .................................................... 52, 53
chicken ............................. 21, 22, 23, 24, 25, 26, 27, 28, 61
chicken breasts ............................................ 25, 28
chicken drumsticks ........................................... 25
chicken stock ..................................................... 57
chicken thighs .................................................... 27
chicken wings ......................................... 23, 24, 26
chili flakes .......................................................... 53
chili powder ....................................................... 27
chives ............................................................ 59, 61
chocolate chips ................................................. 52
chopped almonds ............................................. 50
chopped hazelnuts ........................................... 52
cilantro ............................................................... 58
cinnamon .............................. 25, 49, 50, 51, 52, 55
cinnamon powder .............................. 46, 50, 51
coarse salt .......................................................... 46
cocoa powder .................................................... 46
coconut ............................ 21, 23, 24, 25, 26, 27, 28, 46, 49, 50, 52, 55, 57, 60
coconut cream ............................................ 27, 59
coconut extract ................................................. 46
coconut flour ............................... 27, 28, 46, 57, 60
coconut milk .............................................. 49, 55
coconut oil ..................... 21, 23, 24, 26, 46, 49, 50, 52, 55, 59, 60
coconut shred .................................................... 25
coriander ........................................................... 23
corn .................................................................... 55
Cornish hens ...................................................... 21
corn kernels ....................................................... 48
cream cheese ..................................................... 61
cream of celery soup ........................................ 54
cumin powder ................................................... 54
curry leaves ....................................................... 47

## D
dark chocolate .................................................. 53
dark chocolate chips ........................................ 53
dried basil .......................................................... 24
dried cherries .................................................... 49
dried cilantro ..................................................... 58
dried cranberries .............................................. 49
dried figs ............................................................ 50
dried parsley ...................................................... 57
dry mustard ....................................................... 51

## E
egg ............................. 25, 27, 28, 46, 48, 49, 50, 51, 53, 54, 55, 57, 59, 60
eggnog ............................................................... 50
Erythritol ........................................................... 24

## F
fig ....................................................................... 50
flax meal ............................................................ 60
flax seeds ..................................................... 53, 55
fresh cilantro ..................................................... 47
fresh Italian herbs ...................................... 48, 51
fresh parsley ...................................................... 47

## G
Gai yang spices .................................................. 21
garlic ............................... 23, 27, 47, 48, 53, 54, 58, 59, 61
garlic powder ........................... 23, 47, 51, 52, 61
ghee ............................................................. 58, 59
ginger ................................................................. 25
green beans ....................................................... 28
ground cloves .............................................. 49, 55

## H
half-and-half ..................................................... 54
hazelnut ............................................................. 52
hazelnuts ........................................................... 28
heavy cream ................................................ 48, 55
heavy whipping cream .................................... 58
honey ................................................................. 49

**64** | The Korean Home Kitchen

## I
instant coffee granules .................................................. 46
Italian parsley leaves ..................................................... 54
Italian seasoning .................................................... 51, 61

## J
jasmine rice .................................................................... 52

## K
keto BBQ sauce ............................................................. 26
kosher salt ..................................................................... 49

## L
lemon ..................................................................... 22, 58
lemon juice ............................................................ 22, 58
lemon zest .............................................................. 22, 58
lime zest ........................................................................ 58

## M
macaroni ....................................................................... 51
maple syrup .................................................................. 52
milk .................................................... 46, 49, 50, 51
millet ............................................................................. 55
Monterey Jack cheese ................................................... 61
mozzarella .............................................................. 60, 61
mozzarella cheese ......................................................... 60
multigrain rice ........................................................ 47, 53
mushroom ....................................................... 57, 60, 61
mustard ................................................................. 60, 61

## N
nutmeg ....................................................... 27, 46, 51, 52, 55

## O
old-fashioned oats ............................................... 52, 53, 55
olive oil ............................................ 25, 26, 27, 28, 47, 54, 57, 61
onion ................................................... 25, 26, 47, 48, 53, 54, 57, 60
onion powder ................................................... 25, 26, 60
oregano ................................................................. 27, 28

## P
pancetta ........................................................................ 55
Paneer cheese ............................................................... 54
paprika ................................................... 21, 26, 54, 58
Parmesan cheese .................................................... 48, 55
parsley ................................................... 27, 28, 55
peas ............................................................................... 53
pecan ............................................................................. 53
pesto .............................................................................. 58
pork ............................................................................... 25
pork rinds ..................................................................... 25
Provolone ...................................................................... 27
Provolone cheese .......................................................... 27
prune ............................................................................. 49
pumpkin ........................................................................ 53

## Q
quinoa ........................................................................... 48
quinoa flakes .......................................................... 52, 53

## R
rice .......................................................... 47, 54, 55
rice flour ....................................................................... 54
rolled oats ..................................................................... 46

## S
scallion .................................................................. 47, 52
self-rising flour ............................................................. 46
sesame oil .............................................. 53, 55, 57
shallot ................................................................... 54, 55
slivered almonds ........................................................... 52
sour cream .................................................................... 60
soy sauce ....................................................................... 53
spinach .......................................................................... 61
sugar .............................................................................. 55
Sultanas ......................................................................... 55
sunflower oil ................................................................. 61
sweet corn bread ........................................................... 55
sweet raisin bread ......................................................... 49

## T
taco seasoning ............................................................... 24
thyme ..................................................................... 27, 61
tofu ................................................................................ 58
tomato ........................................................................... 58
turmeric ........................................................................ 58
turmeric powder ........................................................... 57

## U
unsweetened coconut flakes ......................................... 52

## V
vanilla ................................................ 46, 49, 50, 51, 52, 53, 55
vanilla essence .............................................................. 53
vanilla extract ............................................ 46, 49, 50, 51, 52
vegetable broth ....................................................... 47, 52

## W
whole-wheat flour ........................................................ 48

## Z
zucchini ......................................................................... 59

The Korean Home Kitchen | **65**

**BAEK MEE-YON**

Printed in Great Britain
by Amazon